Golden Rules

GOLDEN RULES

*The Ten Ethical Values
Parents Need to Teach
Their Children*

Wayne Dosick

HarperSanFrancisco
A Division of HarperCollins*Publishers*

FIRST EDITION
Set in Granjon

Library of Congress Cataloging-in-Publication Data
Dosick, Wayne D.
Golden rules : the ten ethical values parents need to teach their children /
Wayne Dosick.
    p.   cm.
Includes bibliographical references.
ISBN 0–06–251204–8 (cloth)
ISBN 0–06–251249–8 (pbk)
    1. Children—Conduct of life.   2. Children—Religious life.   3. Child
rearing—Moral and ethical aspects.   4. Moral education.   5. Moral
development.   I. Title.
BJ1631.D66   1995
649'.7—dc20   94–37098
                                                                      CIP
95 96 97 98 99 ❖ RRD(H) 10 9 8 7 6 5 4 3 2 1

This edition is printed on acid-free paper
that meets the American National Standards
Institute Z39.48 Standard.

To the memory of
Alan ז"ל

childhood lost;
childhood reclaimed.

CONTENTS

ACKNOWLEDGMENTS

My deepest thanks and gratitude to:

My parents, Hyman and Roberta Dosick, and my parents-in-law, Clarence and Anna Kaufman, whose life teachings of decency and goodness continually influence and inspire.

My sons, Scott and Seth, for the privilege and joy of being their father.

My colleagues and friends—wise educators, counselors, and spiritual guides—whose professional and personal knowledge and insight have added immeasurably to the ideas and the tone this book: Michele Blumberg, Dr. Steven R. Helfgot, The Rev. James J. O'Leary, S. J., Rabbi David M. Posner, Rabbi Jack Riemer, Sharon Kaplan Roszia, Alan Rubin, Patricia S. Rubin, Dr. Virginia Shabatay, and Dr. Yehuda Shabatay. And our cousin, Estelle Strizhak, who was the "midwife" at the birth and naming of LUMIES.

My esteemed literary agent, Sandra Dijkstra, who keeps the faith; and the fine folks at Harper San Francisco whose company vision honors the world of the spirit. I am especially grateful to my superb editor, Kandace Hawkinson, whose editorial skills are surpassed only by her literary sensitivities and her abiding commitment to a world of justice and goodness.

And most of all, my wife, Ellen—cherished partner, guide, healer, visionary. ". . . and all the women went out after her with timbrels and with dances." (Ex. 15:20)

"Every living being gives thanks to You;
parents tell children of Your gracious acts." (Is. 38:19)

*I did not go to the Master
to learn sacred scripture,
but to watch him tie his shoes.*

Chasidic saying

Teach your children well.

Deuteronomy 6:7
Crosby, Stills, Nash & Young, 1969

IN THE BEGINNING

As we were walking out of the stadium after watching a San Diego Padres baseball game, I casually but purposefully moved my wallet from the back pocket to the front pocket of my pants.

My then-young son noticed what I had done and asked, "Hey, Dad, why did you put your wallet in your other pocket?"

I—who had grown up being jostled by the crowds coming out of Comiskey Park and Wrigley Field in Chicago—replied, "Well, Scott, if someone wants to steal my wallet, it's much harder to take it from my front pocket than from my back pocket."

And my puzzled son—a child of the "golden ghetto" of sunny Southern California—asked in all innocence and with all seriousness, "But who would want to steal your wallet?"

"The Times, They Are A'Changin' "

It was a simpler world—even those fifteen years ago when my boys were growing up—and a far less complicated time when we, their parents, were kids ourselves.

In his nationally syndicated column, noted social commentator Ken Adelman (who grew up in the same south side Chicago neighborhood at the same time I did) reported on a widely published survey, in an article which he entitled, "Why Do Americans Feel So Bad?"

In the early 1950s, elementary school teachers from across the United States were asked to list the top five problems in their schools. They replied:

1. talking out of turn
2. chewing gum
3. making noise
4. running in the hall
5. cutting in line

In the early 1990s, the same question was asked of teachers. Their replies were profoundly different:

1. drug and alcohol abuse
2. guns and knives in school
3. pregnancy
4. suicide
5. rape

More than three-quarters of all Americans believe that this country is in serious moral and spiritual decline.

It's no wonder!

Police report that in a recent twelve-month period, more than 1.7 million young people under the age of eighteen were arrested for criminal activity.

By most estimates, more than 1.5 million children in America come to school every day carrying a weapon.

Not long ago, on a school playground, a twelve-year-old boy shot a seven-year-old girl to death because she was, according to the boy's dispassionate and self-righteous explanation, "dissing" him (showing him disrespect) because she was standing on his shadow.

Less devastating but equally disturbing is the report that more than two-thirds of American teenagers claim that when they are adults, they will have absolutely no moral qualms about padding their business expense accounts or cheating on their taxes.

No one is immune.

Bewilderment and fear cut deeply into *every* racial, ethnic, and socioeconomic group.

Crime and violence, poverty and despair have robbed an entire generation of inner-city children of the innocence and security of childhood.

Mistrust and alienation, ennui and nihilism have seeped into suburbia, so that even children of wealth and privilege drift without purpose or direction.

Like Alice who fell down the rabbit hole, many of our children live in a world turned upside down. They swirl, topsy-turvy, in a chaotic abyss, and we—who are to be their guides and their protectors —ache to save them, but we do not seem to know how.

The very soul of contemporary society weeps in confusion and pain.

Why?

Many are quick to assign blame.

Some children, it is claimed, have too little.

Some of our children lack a social value system and an ethical core because of (choose one or more) economic deprivation, racial discrimination, readily available alcohol and drugs, absent fathers, neighborhoods that have become battlegrounds, and schools that have become empty shells of hopelessness.

Some children, it is claimed, never have quite enough.

Some of our children—the children of economic necessity or lifestyle choice—act out their fears and frustrations because (choose one or more) they spend most of their waking hours in sterile day-care centers; they eat too many of their meals off government-sponsored trays; they spend their weekends shuttling between the homes of their divorced—and often warring—parents; and their most frequent playmates are Big Bird and Barney.

Some children, it is claimed, have too much.

Some of our children misbehave and lack direction because (choose one or more) they spend more time each year sitting in front of a television set rather than sitting in a schoolroom; their senses are being bombarded by lurid music lyrics and their minds are being numbed by senseless video games; and their affluent parents isolate them in exclusive private schools and camps, and spoil them with every manner of material possession.

Yet, whatever their background or circumstance—poor or rich, exalted or ignoble, privileged or deprived—there are children who rise up above their origins, who prevail over their environment, who conquer their personal "dragons," and become good, decent, honorable human beings, with strength of character and depth of moral commitment.

Why?

Why do some people and not others choose a life of goodness and decency?

You've Got Their Whole World in Your Hands

There is but one real way that children get the moral bearings and develop the inner fortitude to have and sustain an ethical value system that defines their lives.

Despite an occasional government program, despite a special neighbor, teacher or coach, despite a motivating priest, minister, rabbi, or imam, **it is parents who give children a value system, a sense of morality, and an ethical standard.**

Your children need a clear set of moral values by which to lead their lives. They need to know how to behave and how to conduct their everyday encounters. They need to know how to act when the choices they make affect and impact on others. They need to know the difference between right and wrong. **And it is you—their parents—who, through your love and devoted commitment, can teach your children the good, the decent, the right way to live.**

From Where Will Your Help Come?

Being a parent—being entrusted with guarding and shaping a human life—has never been an easy task.

And in the climate of contemporary America, with its moral compass askew, being a parent who guides wisely and well is more difficult than ever.

Where are you to find the ethical standards, the code of moral behavior, to teach your children? And, then, how do you best convey to them your most cherished and precious values?

In the same syndicated column where he reported the teachers' lament, Ken Adelman offered what might be the best hope for a source of guidance and direction. "Turning back to religion," he wrote, "aids the social fabric. Over time, it can alter those behavior problems the 1990 teachers identified. . . . Religion, after all, provides us with moral bearings."

Yet while the vast majority of Americans report that they believe in God or a universal spirit, fewer than three in ten regularly attend formal religious services. Contemporary society is unlikely to return to religious observance as it was once practiced.

What is needed is a reawakening and a recommitment to religion's core teachings: the basic values of human existence—the standards of ethical behavior that define and "make or break" a human being: the virtues of respect, honesty, fairness, responsibility, compassion, gratitude, friendship, peace, maturity, and faith.

It does not matter whether you are a "believer" or if you belong to an organized religious group. For, as Mahatma Gandhi put it, "God has no religion."

What matters is that the world's spiritual traditions—rooted in ancient and eternal wisdom—have much to teach you. They have a deep and enduring knowledge to impart to you about how you—and your children—can be the best you can be.

When you speak to your children from the place of spirit, you can teach them that leading a life of moral goodness is the finest expression and the grandest celebration of the human mind and heart.

You can teach your children that ethical law—the way by which we human beings tame our passions through self-discipline—is the human spirit at its best: enlightened, empowered, and enabled; free to make choices; balancing the obligations of responsibility with maintaining personal rights; considering the common good while protecting special interests.

You can teach your children that ethical law is the human spirit at its most free, for the ultimate moral courage is the freedom to say, "no."

To Guide and Illumine

Bringing up ethical children is not about having "good" children who clean their plates and clean their rooms—though these are, certainly, desirable and valuable behaviors. **Rather, bringing up ethical children is training your sons and daughters to do good, to do right; to be decent and honorable and righteous;** to be—in the Yiddish word that has become such a well-understood part of the English language—a *mensch*—a genuine, faithful, worthy, humane human being.

Golden Rules is a guidebook to the moral values most needed by today's children. Embracing and "owning" these ten golden rules of ethical behavior will give your children the solid foundation to lead lives of goodness and decency.

Golden Rules is also a very practical handbook, for interspersed in each chapter—and easily distinguishable in their bordered boxes—are fifty **LUMIES.**

LUMIES—which illumine and enlighten—are simple, everyday ways of conveying ethical values to your children.

LUMIES are helpful suggestions and action-oriented activities, which you can easily make part of your daily life, to teach and model ethical behavior.

Like any other ability or skill, value-based morality and ethical behavior can be taught when the teacher is caring and committed, firm, and, at the same time, gentle.

At the end of each chapter in the *Golden Rules* is a story to tell your children. Tell the stories over and over again, for stories seep into the consciousness—and the conscience—and reverberate and resonate for a long, long time.

Then, each chapter has three questions to discuss with your children: one question for your children, ages four to eight; one for your youngsters, ages nine to twelve; and one for your teenagers. Each question presents a real-life moral dilemma for your children to face and asks them to consider their choices.

You can use these questions as a "springboard" for discussions with your children—to give you the opportunity to share your beliefs with them; to give them a safe place to develop their principles and values; to help them form their moral character; and to teach them how to make their own ethical decisions.

And at the very end of each chapter is a prayer for you to recite with your children, for a family that prays together creates sacred space and holy moments, and sends out to the universe—and back to each soul—life-affirming, life-enhancing energy.

A Personal Word

In this book, you will occasionally read stories about my sons, Scott and Seth—and, in most cases, my boys will seem to be pretty good kids. I tell you these stories not because my children—who are now adults themselves—are any better than any other children, but because these are the children I know most intimately.

Scott and Seth are not my children by birth—I married their mother when they were four and two years old—but we became father and sons through life and love, and, eventually, law.

Yet, all was far from perfect.

As a rabbi who spent so many of his waking hours working with other people's children, I cannot help but wonder if I spent enough time and energy with my own.

There were—from both parents and children—the usual frustrations and disappointments; there was more than one father-son confrontation. More than once, I despaired that my children were rejecting the values that I hold most dear.

And there was trauma. Their mother and I are no longer married, so they lived through the arguments and the pain of a faltering marriage, and learned that their parents are less than perfect, and that life is not always fair or fun.

I tell you all these things so that you will know, right from the very beginning, that when I talk to you about teaching children ethical values, I am neither a disengaged observer nor an impartial academic researcher. I am a parent—just like you—who tried the best I knew how, and learned as much, and more, from my failures as from my successes.

By parenting—steeped in spiritual teachings and committed to conveying eternal values—I learned, most of all, that children trust honesty, respect sincerity, appreciate vulnerability, and honor heartfelt conviction.

Now, the butterflies fly free, and I can only marvel at their brilliant colors.

With All Your Heart

Not long ago, a world-famous educator was asked to consult with a state agency on the building of a new facility for troubled and delinquent children.

He looked over the agency's plans, and he wrote a report that strongly suggested upgrading everything in the original proposal. The dormitories and the classrooms should be outfitted with state-of-the-art fixtures; the sports fields should have the finest equipment; the educational program should utilize the newest innovative techniques and be supplied with the most up-to-date materials; the kitchen should serve quality meals; the most experienced staff should be hired.

The consultant concluded his report by writing, "If only one child is saved from a life of moral decay, it will justify all the costs and the labor invested in this facility."

The director of the state agency thanked the educator for his work, but said, "I wish that we could afford to implement all your suggestions, but, after all, this is a publicly funded project, and our monies are limited. But, tell me, didn't you get just a bit carried away? Would all these costs really be justified if we could save only *one* child?"

And the educator replied, "If it were *my* child, yes!"

It is your children—your precious sons and daughters—who can be guided to a life of moral decency and ethical goodness when you choose to teach them and model for them.

The modern axiom teaches, "There are only two lasting things we can give our children. One is roots. The other is wings."

Giving the gift of roots and wings is a challenge and a commitment worthy of every fiber of your being—"all your heart, all your soul, all your might."

It is this gift that fulfills the promise you made to yourself and to your precious children when you decided to bring them into the world. And it is this gift that fulfills your stake in human history.

Your children, their troubled world, and—most of all—their destinies, are waiting.

In the question of the ancient sage, "If not now, when?"

———⬯———

*"Honor Your Father and
Your Mother"*

The Ethic of RESPECT

A mother, father, and their seven-year-old daughter were seated in a restaurant. The waitress first took the order from the adults, and, then, she turned to the little girl.

"What will you have?" she asked.

The little girl looked timidly at her parents and, then, said to the waitress, "I'll have a hot dog on a bun."

"No hot dog," said her mother. "She'll have a nice piece of roasted chicken."

"With mashed potatoes and vegetables," added her father.

The waitress kept looking straight at the little girl and she asked, "Would you like ketchup or mustard on your hot dog?"

"Mustard, please," replied the girl.

"Coming right up," said the waitress, as she headed toward the kitchen.

The family sat in stunned silence. Finally, the little girl looked at her parents and said, "You know what? She thinks that I am real!"

Of Dust and Divinity

A life of goodness and decency begins with the recognition of the infinite worth of each and every human being.

The psalmist of old looked at the immense, grand universe in which he lived and was moved to awe: "O Lord, the world is filled with the greatness of Your glory. The heavens display Your splendor. The cries of infants attest to Your power."

Yet, in the midst of this vast grandeur, he wondered about his place: "When I see the heavens, Your handiwork, the moon and the stars which You have formed, I ask, 'What are we that You should be mindful of us—mere human beings that You should take notice of us?' "

The psalmist's answer to his own question gives him—and us—comfort and joy: "You have made us almost Divine. You have crowned us with honor and glory. You have given us sway over all Your works. O Lord, the world *is* filled with the greatness of Your glory."

In every human being, there is a spark of the Divine, an image of the Eternal.

Knowing this, of course, could be cause for conceit and arrogance. But, just as assuredly, it can be cause for confidence and faith.

That is why an old legend teaches that every person should have two pockets. In one pocket should be a piece of paper on which is written, "I am but dust and ashes." In the other pocket should be a piece of paper on which is written, "For my sake alone was the world created."

When a person is feeling too proud, he should take the paper from the first pocket and read it: "I am but dust and ashes."

When a person is feeling disheartened or lowly, she should take the paper from the second pocket and read it: "For my sake alone was the world created."

We are the joining together of two worlds. Of dust we were fashioned, but our spirit is the breath of the Divine.

When you teach your children to see the value and worth of every human being, when you teach your children to honor and respect the uniqueness of each person, then you teach your children to see the Divine spark within everyone—and to touch the Divine spark within themselves.

In Family

Even though reality is radically different now, you may still—like so many other of today's parents—carry with you the fantasy image of the "ideal" American family.

Television's *Ozzie and Harriet* and *Leave It to Beaver* portrayed the mythical "perfect" family: a working father, a stay-at-home mother, two children, and two cars—one, of course, a station wagon with wood paneling on the sides—parked in the driveway of a suburban house, with a basketball hoop on the garage and a dog frolicking on the front lawn.

Loving parents and children—unfazed by life's everyday realities and undaunted by major challenges or minor conflicts—easily solved life's little problems with nonchalance and gentle humor, in thirty minutes or less.

We know that these kinds of families are little more than the creative imagination of Hollywood script writers.

In reality, families—forged as much in love and experience as in biology—come in all forms and configurations.

Yet, one thing about families remains unchanging and constant.

In family, children grow and learn how to be the adults they will eventually become by modeling themselves after the adults in their lives.

Eat Breakfast

It's a rough world out there—even for your kids. The pressures to succeed, fierce competition, petty jealousies, the burning desire to be more attractive and popular, are not just "grown-up" problems, but reach into every classroom, and onto every sports field and playground.

Even in the morning rush to get everyone to school on time, in clean clothes and brushed hair, with book bags and lunch boxes packed, find the time to spend five or seven minutes with your children at the breakfast table.

Talk and—more importantly—listen.

Your children will know that they are important to you, and your presence and attention will provide the confidence, trust, support, and love that it takes to get through the day.

Watching You

In family, your children will learn, first, how they are to treat people by watching how you treat people.

And their most impressionable lessons will come from how *you* treat *them*.

If you dismiss your children because they are "only children," or if you ignore them because "children should be seen but not heard," they will feel overlooked and unimportant. If you regard your children only as "pride-producing machines"—you know, "the doctor is three years old and the lawyer is two"—they will measure their worth by *what they do*, not by *who they are*.

To treat each and every person they meet with decency and dignity, your children need to be imbued with a strong, solid sense of self. For only a person with self-respect can respect others, and only a person who feels honored can honor another.

So, if you continually demonstrate your love for your children by appreciating and validating them, if you listen to their ideas and acknowledge their feelings, they will—at the core of their beings—feel safe and secure, valuable and esteemed, respected and respectable.

Then, they will be able to respect and honor others.

As the poet put it, "What the mother sings to the cradle goes all the way down to the coffin."

And, in family, by watching how their parents behave and treat others—as men and women, as husbands and wives, as lovers, as partners, as friends, and as loving beings—children learn about their own nature: their sexuality, their role in life, their capacity for communion, for intimacy, and for love.

Every year at Christmastime, many are drawn back to O. Henry's story *The Gift of the Magi,* because it so wonderfully demonstrates not only the spirit of the season, but the human spirit of love and devotion. It shows us a partnership of selflessness and self-sacrifice. It shows us how a lovely, highly feminine woman can touch her strength and power, and how an extremely masculine man can touch his gentleness and compassion.

In the story, Jim and Della, young and deeply in love, very much want to buy each other beautiful gifts for Christmas. But they are poor; they have no money for expensive presents.

Jim's most prized possession is his gold pocket watch, an heirloom passed from his grandfather to his father to him. Yet he sells his watch to have the money to buy Della her gift—exquisite tortoise-shell combs for her long, luxurious hair.

At the same time, Della cuts off her hair and sells it, in order to have the money to buy Jim his gift—a gold chain for his pocket watch.

Praise People

It can be so easy to see the worst in people: to criticize and judge, to malign and condemn, to gossip and bear tales.

But, it is so much better to see the best in people: to find favor and express approval, to extol and acclaim their virtues.

Rather than letting your children hear you speaking harsh or mean words about anyone, let your words be full of praise—sweet and gentle.

When you avoid using derogatory or slang "labels" to refer to any person, when you avoid telling ethnic or racial jokes, your children will know that although stereotypes and caricatures may elicit a laugh, they are not funny, for they diminish and demean the human spirit.

When you continually demonstrate that the honor of every person is as precious to you as your own, your children will learn how to affirm and celebrate the dignity and the worth of each and every human being.

Whether you are married, in a partnership, or are single, you can teach your children what it means to be a man, what it means to be a woman, what it takes to be emotionally solid and self-sufficient, and what it takes to be successful in an intimate relationship by how you claim your sense of self; by how you display your internal and external strengths and tenderness; by how you balance your personal power and your deep compassion.

You teach your children to make the life of another as precious as their own when you are selfless and generous, giving and kind.

When you love deeply and demonstrably, your example will extend far. When your children see adults respect, care for, and love each other, they learn not only how to behave in their personal and most intimate relationships, but how to respect, care about, and love *all* people.

As the noted psychologist Dr. Erich Fromm taught, "love is . . . an attitude, an orientation of character which determines the relatedness of a person to the world as a whole. . . . If I truly love one person, I love all persons, I love the world, I love life."

Honor Deserved; Honor Given

Haifa, a coastal city in the north of Israel, boasted of the country's only subway. The entire system was made up of but three stops— one at the port, one half-way up the city's mountainous terrain, and one at the very top of the mountain.

Stenciled on the walls of each of the cars was what appeared, at first, to be typical subway graffiti, but was, actually, a message from the operators.

The words—taken from the biblical book of Leviticus—said, "You shall rise before the aged." Practically, they served as a simple instruction: "Get up and give your seat to an older person."

Yet, the injunction means so much more, for it is rooted in the great sense of respect and honor, which every spiritual tradition accords the elderly.

Attaining length of years means having accumulated a lifetime of learning and wisdom. Reaching old age means having been forged by experience and having been tempered by success and failure, tragedy and triumph. That is why the heads of so many tribes and churches are called "elders"—wise leaders capable of giving guidance, direction, and good counsel.

Yet so much of modern society—reflected, especially, in the advertising and marketing of commercial products—disdains aging, and rejects anything and anyone old, celebrating, instead, that which is new, fresh, young, nubile.

Speak Love; Show Love

You may have love in your heart; you may have love in your thoughts. But, your children are not mind readers.

Unless you *tell* your children, unless you *show* your children, they may never know how very much you love them.

Every day—many times every day—say, "I love you." Say it over and over again, so that your children hear, and know, and are sure.

And, touch your children. Hold their hands. Hug them. Kiss them. Cuddle with them. Have them lean their heads on your shoulder. Let them feel your warmth enveloping them, and protecting them, and loving them.

There is nothing your children want more than your love, and nothing is more satisfying—and reassuring—than when they feel your loving touch and hear your loving words.

A poignant poem portrays the anguish of the elderly who feel ignored and dismissed.

An elderly woman, being cared for in an old age home, asks, "What do you see, nurses, what do you see? What are you thinking when you look at me?"

The woman thinks that the nurses see her only as a crabby old woman with a far-away look, who dribbles her food and loses her shoe, who does the nurses' bidding, and eats at their will.

But, she knows that they are not seeing who she really is. She fondly and joyfully remembers her life: as a small child with a loving mother and father, brothers and sisters; as a young girl in love; as a devoted bride; as a mother herself; as a grandmother; and, then, as a widow with her husband gone and her children living far away.

"I'm an old woman now and nature is cruel. 'Tis her jest to make old age look like a fool. The body crumbles, grace and vigor depart. . . . But inside this carcass, a young girl still dwells."

So, she cries out, "Open your eyes, nurses, open and see—not a crabby old woman. Look closer. See ME!"

You bring your children to the deepest level of respect for all people when you teach them the enduring and special value of the aging and the elderly.

In the way your children see you treating your own parents—in the way that they see you following the biblical command to "honor your father and your mother"—they will learn to respect and honor the elderly, and, in turn, they will imitate you and observe the rule to honor their father and mother—you—when you are old.

There was an old man who lived in his son's house. Life was very pleasant for him: he had his own room, with ample space for all his things; his son and daughter-in-law treated him well; there was a young grandson in whom he took great delight.

Every evening, the family gathered around a large round table for dinner. There, they shared good food and quiet conversation. The man was happy and content.

As the years went by, the old man's health began to fail. His hands began to shake, and, sometimes, because of his trembling hands, he would spill his tea or drop his plate.

With each spill, the son became more and more upset with his father.

One evening, as the family sat around the dinner table, the man accidentally hit his bowl with his soup spoon, and the bowl broke, spilling soup all over the table.

The man's son jumped up from his place and shouted at his father, "What's wrong with you? You are so clumsy. If you can't

Visit the Elderly

Take your children to visit older folks—their grandparents, neighbors, members of the church, synagogue or mosque, residents of an old age home—as often as you can.

Children whose own grandparents are nearby will make even more friends over the "generational leap." Children whose own grandparents may be no longer living, or who may live far away, can "adopt" a grandparent.

The elderly whom you visit can have new friends and "honorary" grandchildren.

Watch how comfortable your children and these elderly folks quickly become with each other. Watch your children see not age or infirmity, but real human beings.

Watch the magic sparkle between the generations as understanding and trust, mutual respect, love and commitment bloom and grow.

Given the opportunity and the place, together, "your young shall dream dreams and your old shall see visions."

eat properly at our table, you will have to eat alone in your room. I'm tired of you spilling food and breaking our good dishes."

The next day, the son brought home a wooden bowl, and, from then on, the old man ate his dinner in his own room, out of his wooden bowl. He said nothing to his son or daughter-in-law, but being away from his family at dinnertime pained him very much.

One day, when the son came home from work, he found his young boy sitting at the workbench in the garage, quietly working on a project.

"What are you making?" he asked.

His young son proudly held up his work. "I am making a wooden bowl. I am carving it all by myself."

"A wooden bowl?" asked his father. "What will you use it for? We already have such beautiful dishes."

And the little boy answered, "I know, Dad, but I'm making this bowl for *you,* when you grow old like Grandpa, and come to live with me. When your hands begin to shake and you break my plates, I'll have this bowl ready for you to use in your room."

When the father heard this, he immediately ran to his own father and fell to his knees. "Father, my father, I am so sorry. Please, please forgive me for not showing you the respect and honor that is rightly yours."

And that night, the whole family sat together again at the big round dining room table.

As You Are

Every moment of every day is the "living laboratory" where your children form their moral underpinnings as they model themselves after you, while watching how you treat the people in your life.

You can model for them with sensitivity and integrity when you remember this story told of the great master, Mahatma Gandhi.

A mother brought her son to Gandhi, and said, "Please, Master, tell my son to stop eating sugar."

Gandhi looked deeply into the boy's eyes, and, then, said to the mother, "Bring your son back to me in two weeks."

"But, Master," she said, "we have come on a long journey to be with you. Please do not send us away. Please tell my son to stop eating sugar."

Once again, Gandhi looked deeply into the boy's eyes but, once again, he said, "Bring your son back to me in two weeks."

Visit the Cemetery

When your grandparents, parents, or others dear to you have died, take your children to visit the cemetery.

Don't go to be sad or melancholy, but, rather, to be in a place of remembrance and tribute—to share with your children your warm memories of the people you love.

Go on a beautiful day—when the sun is shining and the wind is gently blowing.

With tears and smiles—and much, much love—remember your loved ones, and tell your children their stories.

When you take your children to the cemetery, you give them the gift of their history and heritage, their legacy and destiny.

Two weeks later, the mother and son returned. She said, "Please, Master, tell my son to stop eating sugar."

Gandhi looked deeply into the boy's eyes, and said, "Stop eating sugar."

The mother said, "Oh thank you, Master, thank you. But, please tell me. Why did you send us away? Why didn't you tell my son to stop eating sugar two weeks ago when we were here?"

And Gandhi replied, "Two weeks ago, I was eating sugar."

You can model for your children wisely and well when you remember that they will be like the mountain climbers, following the guide up the mountain, who say, "Please be careful. We are walking in your footsteps."

You model for your children best when you always, always remember: **As you are, so will they be.**

A Story to Tell Your Children

The Rice Field

A long, long time ago, in a faraway land called Japan, there was a small village. On one side of the village was the great ocean, and on the other side were high mountains.

A few of the people in the village made their living by fishing, but most of the men, women, and children worked in the rice fields that were high on top of one of the mountains. Every morning, the villagers climbed the mountain path to work. Every evening, they trekked down the mountain to sleep in their huts in the village.

Only a grandmother and her granddaughter—whose name was Hanako—lived on top of the mountain, where it was their job to keep the fires lit at night to scare off the wild animals who might eat the rice.

Early one morning, during the season when the rice fields turned golden and dry, ready for the harvest, Grandmother tended to the fires for one last time. Down below, the villagers began doing their morning chores before climbing the mountain to begin the day's work.

As she did every day after stirring the morning fire, Grandmother went to the mountain's edge to watch the sun rise. But, on this day, she did not see the sun coming up. Instead, what she saw brought her terrible fear.

As quickly as she could, she ran to the hut where her granddaughter was sleeping. "Hanako, " she called, "get up. Get up."

"Oh, Grandmother," said Hanako, "I am tired, please let me sleep."

"No, Hanako. Get up right now, and do as I say. Go get a burning stick from the fire."

Hanako knew that she must do as she was told, for she had never heard her grandmother so excited. Without knowing why, Hanako went to get a burning stick from the fire, and soon she joined her grandmother who was standing near the fields.

Grandmother cried out a command, "Burn the rice fields."

"But, Grandmother," Hanako cried, "we cannot burn the rice fields. This is our village's food. Without this rice, we will all starve."

"Do as I say," commanded her grandmother.

With tears streaming down her face, Hanako did as she was told. She touched her burning stick to the fields and set the precious rice on fire. Soon, huge clouds of black smoke were rising up from the rice fields on the top of the mountain.

Down below, the villagers saw the smoke, and in moments, every man, woman, and child in the village came running up the mountain.

When they reached the top, they could all see the flames destroying their precious rice. Their whole crop was ruined.

"What happened here?" they all cried out. "How did this horrible fire begin?"

"I set the fire," Grandmother told all the villagers.

"What? You set the fire? You stupid old woman! You have ruined our rice crop. We will all starve. How could you do such a stupid thing?"

"Look," said the grandmother, as she pointed out toward the sea. "Look at that fierce storm that is coming toward the shore. In less than an hour, gigantic waves will hit our little village, and everything will be destroyed."

The people stood quietly watching, and before long, they saw that Grandmother was absolutely right. The great storm brought twenty-five-foot-high waves onto the shore, and every hut in the little village was crushed under tons of water.

The villagers looked down at their little village, which lay in ruins, and they looked around at their rice fields that were burned down, and one man cried out, "We have nothing left. Everything is gone. We are ruined."

And every villager moaned and wept.

But one woman said, "All is not lost. We have our lives. Everyone has lived through the storm."

And the village elder said, "That is right, my children, we have the gift of life. So, this afternoon, we will start all over again. We will build new huts, and we will plant new fields.

"But, first, we must thank Grandmother. Far from being a stupid old woman, as some of us have called her, she is really very wise and brave. Grandmother saved all our lives. For, if we had not seen the clouds of smoke from the fires she set in the fields, we would not have run up the mountain so quickly, and we would have been trapped by the waters of the storm."

And for the rest of her life, Grandmother was honored by the villagers for her wisdom and her courage.

Questions to Discuss with Your Children About Respect

A Question to Discuss with Your Children (Ages 4–8)

When you are playing at your best friend's house, her mother always yells and is mean to you.

What do you say? What do you do?

A Question to Discuss with Your Youngsters (Ages 9–12)

You are a very good soccer player, but you spend most of your time sitting on the bench, while your coach plays teammates— especially his son and his friends—who are not as good as you.

How do you convince the coach to give you the playing time you deserve?

A Question to Discuss with Your Teenagers

Your history teacher is dull and boring, wears weird clothes, and has bad breath. Your friends are planning to harass the teacher by purposely misbehaving in class and by spreading rumors about her personal life.

Do you participate in the "campaign" to "get the teacher"? Why? Why not? What do you say to your friends?

A Prayer About Respecting One Another

We thank You, O God
for the gift of our family,
and for the home where we share our lives.

Help us make our home into a holy place,
with family bonds that are loving and strong.

Help us to see the good in all people,
and to honor their lives as our own.

Bless us, all of us together,
with the light of Your presence,
and with Your love.

Amen.

Inspired by Rabbi Sidney Greenberg;
adapted by W. D.

The 2ND

GOLDEN RULE

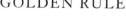

"Be Heedful of Your Words;
Do What Is Right"

The Ethic of
HONESTY

When Bobby was five, he and his father went for a drive in
the country. At a crossroads, Bobby's father drove right
through the red light, without bothering to stop.

Bobby said, "Daddy, in school my teacher taught us that
we are supposed to stop at every red light."

His father replied, "Oh, don't worry son. There's no traf-
fic on this road, and besides, there are no police cars around.
No one will ever see us going through the red light."

When Bobby was twelve, his mother took him to the
movies. As they were going into the theater, she said, "Bobby,
if the usher asks how old you are, say that you are eleven. I
bought you a child's ticket."

When Bobby was sixteen, he overheard his father on the
phone with the family accountant. "That's right, Charlie,"
said Bobby's father, "forget that I ever told you about that
extra income from the stock option deal. There's no record of
it anywhere, so it makes no sense to pay the extra tax."

When Bobby was eighteen, he went off to the state uni-
versity. Six months later, his parents received this letter from
the dean of the college:

Dear Mr. and Mrs. Smith,

I regret to inform you that your son Robert has been expelled from our university. He violated our school's honor code when he was caught cheating on his midterm exam.

Bobby's mother cried out, "Bobby? Cheating on an exam? How could it be? We brought him up in a good home. Where did he ever learn to cheat?"

And Bobby's father sighed, and shook his head, and sadly asked, "How could Bobby do this to us?"

Words of Truth

An ethical person tells the truth, for his word is his bond, and her bond is her honor.

You teach your children to tell the truth when you are heedful of your own words.

There was once a newspaper reporter who came upon the scene of an accident. A large crowd completely surrounded the victim, so that the reporter could not get close enough to see him or the extent of the injuries.

But, the reporter had to get the story, so he shouted out, "I am the father of the victim. Please let me through."

The crowd parted and let him pass, so that he was able to get right up to the scene of the accident—only to discover that the victim was a puppy dog.

When your children learn to tell the truth, they will never be embarrassed by their lies.

The late Speaker of the United States House of Representatives, Sam Rayburn, was once asked, "Mr. Speaker, you see hundreds of people a day. You tell each one 'yes,' 'no,' or 'maybe.' You never make notes of what you have told them, but I have never heard of you forgetting your promise or commitment. What is your secret to remembering what you have said to all the people you meet each day?"

Speaker Rayburn replied, "If you tell the truth, you don't have to remember."

When your children learn to tell the truth, they will never be caught in their lies.

As Jesus taught, "The truth shall make you free."

Words of Goodness

By being heedful of your words, you teach your children that an ethical person does not gossip, or spread rumors, or speak with malice.

The story is told of three clergymen who were out in a boat in the middle of the lake for a day of fishing,

One of them said to his friends, "Here we are, far away from our congregations and the people we serve, far away from our sacred duties. Let's be completely honest with each other, and confess our worst sin. I, for example, like all the things that money can buy. But, my meager salary is never enough to get all the things I want. So every once in a while, I skim some money from the collection plate."

The second clergyman said, "Well, as long as we are being honest with each other, I'll tell you. My sin is gambling. I will place a bet on anything—a baseball game, a football game and, especially, a horse race."

The third clergyman was silent. Finally, his friends said to him, "We have confessed our greatest sins. Now it is your turn. Tell us, what is your greatest vice?"

And the third clergyman said, "My greatest sin is the sin of gossip. And I can hardly wait to get home."

At an early age, children can learn that their **heedless words can do much harm.**

Have you ever been in the summer camp cabin of a group of nine-year-old boys? Have you ever been at a slumber party of thirteen-year-old girls? The way they talk about each other—and, especially about their friends and acquaintances who are not present—can be cutting, vicious, and cruel. And the objects of their words—the youngsters of whom they speak—often later hear what was said about them and never forget.

Once evil words have been spoken, they can never be retrieved. They feed on themselves and fester, and become worse and worse the longer they are exposed. They take on lives of their own and leave damage and destruction in their path.

Therapists' offices are filled with people who are in anguish about words spoken to them or about them. Sometimes the words float in conscious memory, heard over and over again as a drumbeat of anguish. Sometimes they rest just below the surface, resurrected now and then to mock and taunt. Sometimes they are buried deeply in the subconscious, but their tentacles of harm can strangle even the most unsuspecting victim.

Slander and gossip, rumor, innuendo, and character assassination are not victimless crimes. Words do not just dissipate into thin air. They come home to roost, to affront and harass.

You can teach your children to carefully heed their words and respect the reputation of another as dearly as their own when you teach them the lesson of the proverb, "Where there is no wood, the fire goes out; so where there is no talebearer, strife ceases."

Words of Trust

When you are heedful of your words, you can teach your children to trust.

When my son, Seth, was five or six years old, he liked to roller-skate on the sidewalk in front of our house. One of his favorite activities was to start at the top of our driveway and skate downhill, gathering as much speed as possible on the way.

One day, just as I was coming home from a walk in the neighborhood, I saw Seth start down from the top of the driveway, and

Play "Telephone"

Gather your children and some of their friends, seat them all in a big circle, and teach them how to play the game of "Telephone."

You whisper something to the first person in the circle. That person whispers what you have said to the next person; that person to the next; that to the next; until the message has gone all around the circle, whispered from person to person.

You know what will happen. The words and the message will get completely garbled and changed, and will in no way resemble the original words that you whispered to the first person.

Your children and their friends will learn the importance of words because even the simplest words, in the most playful of circumstances, can become distorted and take on whole new meanings. They will learn to speak thoughtfully and carefully because they will understand the power and the potential of the words of their mouths.

—only a few skate strokes into his journey—begin to lose his balance.

Instinctively, he reached out his arms for anything to hold on to, and he grabbed the closest thing—the side view mirror of my car. With a resounding "thunk," he pulled the mirror right off the car, fell down, and landed hard on the concrete.

I rushed up to him, and saw that he wasn't hurt, and, then, without any reason—and certainly without thinking—I began to yell. "How could you grab on to my mirror and pull it right off my car? You just ruined a perfectly good mirror. It will probably cost a hundred bucks to fix it. What's wrong with you?"

Seth began to cry.

Almost immediately, I realized my foolishness. What was wrong with *me*? Why was I yelling at a six-year-old kid who was just trying to protect himself and keep from getting hurt by reaching out for the sturdiest object at hand? Why should I be mad at him? It wasn't his fault the mirror came off. If I wanted to be angry, I should be angry at the car company for making a mirror so flimsy that it could be so easily pulled off by a little kid.

I felt very badly for yelling at Seth for no good reason, and I apologized as best as I could.

As the days and months went by, I forgot about the incident.

But, obviously, Seth did not.

Years later—when he was already in college—Seth reminded me that I had been angry with him for pulling the mirror off my car. "You weren't fair," he said. "You yelled at me for something that wasn't my fault. You hurt my feelings when I was already hurting from falling on the driveway."

The words I had spoken—which I really did not mean—hurt my son and brought him pain. Even if it were ever so slightly, I diminished my child's trust in me, for, in his mind, if I could be so unfair once, I might be just as intemperate again.

My heedless words rippled far and were remembered for a long, long time.

Your words have the power to affirm or shatter your children's world and to teach them to trust or doubt.

"I know that I promised you that we would play catch tonight, my son. But, I'm so tired. I just can't do it. You understand, don't you? But don't worry. I promise. We'll play tomorrow night, as soon as I get home from work. I promise."

"I know that I promised you that I would be at your dance recital, my daughter. But, my meeting ran late. And, then, my boss insisted on speaking to me. And, then, traffic was just horrible on the way home. You understand, don't you? But don't worry. I promise. I'll be at your very next recital. That's six months from now, right? I'll be there. I promise."

Your words have the power to elevate or crush your children's well-being and to teach them to love or loathe themselves and the people around them.

What do your children hear you say to them?

When they hear you say, "I love you. You are a great kid. I'm so proud of you. I'm so happy for you"—they believe you, and remember.

And when they hear you say, "How could you do such a thing? Can't you ever do anything right? You must be the dumbest kid in the whole world. How did I get such a stupid child? You'll never amount to anything"—they believe you, and remember.

Your words echo for a long, long time.

When you are tempted to speak words that may hurt or harm, that may bring misunderstanding or mistrust, you can join in the words of the prayer that asks, "Guard my tongue from evil and my lips from speaking guile," for you know that "there are those whose words pierce like a sword, but the tongue of the wise has the powers of redemption."

Honest Dealings

When I was growing up, my father owned a small chain of independent grocery stores on Chicago's south side.

By the time I was seven or eight years old, I was allowed to "work" in the stores. At first, I learned to bag groceries at the end of the check-out line and help customers carry the bags to their cars. When I got a little older, I was allowed to sell candy and gum from the counter. When I got bigger, I learned to put the canned goods on the shelves and the frozen foods into the refrigerated cases. Still later, I learned to work the cash register and make

Play "Truth or Dare"

Challenge your children to a game of "Truth or Dare."

The rules are simple. One player asks another, "truth or dare?"—meaning, "when I ask you a question, will you tell me the truth, or would you rather perform a 'dare,' a stunt which I devise for you?"

By playing this game, you get to hear your children's truths—their choices, their ethical decisions, their moral "bottom line"—and they get to hear—and be influenced by—yours.

In the most nonthreatening—and fun—ways, your children give you the chance to guide them toward wise moral choices, and give you the place to help shape their ethical values.

From your truths, theirs will come.

---

change. Finally, when I was in high school, I was "promoted" to work in the produce department—to set out the fruits and vegetables in beautiful displays and to fill the customers' special orders.

It was there, in the produce department, that I learned the "Hyman Dosick (he's my father) cherry rule."

The "cherry rule" is a simple combination of great marketing and meticulous honesty.

If you put a pound of cherries—even, by scale weight, *more* than a pound—into a container that can hold two pounds of cherries, the customers think that they are being cheated. But, if you put a pound of cherries—a *full* scale weight pound—into a container that is made to hold only three-quarters of a pound, then the customers think that they are getting a great deal.

It makes sense. Even if it contains the exact same pound of cherries, an overflowing container is much more appealing—and will sell much better—than a half-full container.

But, the key to the "cherry rule" is not the marketing allure of an overflowing container. It is the scrupulous weighing of the cherries to assure that a full pound is in the container.

It would be easy to leave out a few cherries, to short-weigh the container. There seems to be so much fruit in the box that no one would ever think that any cherries are missing. But, unless the weight is full and complete, the marketing technique is no longer a sales tool but a dishonest ploy that cheats the customer.

"If you are ever tempted," my father always told his employees—including me—"to leave out a few cherries, short-weigh the container, and short-change the customer, ask yourself what will happen if the assessor from the Department of Weights and Measures comes to hold a surprise inspection of the cherry containers you have packed. Will you be praised for your complete honesty, or will you be cited for cheating?"

And then—from his own beliefs and life-perspective—my father always added, "The ultimate Assessor—your conscience and your God—is always watching and inspecting you—not only when you pack the cherry boxes, but in everything you do."

The "Hyman Dosick cherry rule" applies not just to the fruit market. **For you can teach your children that an ethical person is honest in every act, every deed, every dealing.**

As the old axiom teaches, "There are no degrees of honesty. Either you are honest or you are not."

The Consequences of Dishonesty

You can teach your children what it means to be an ethical person when you show them how dishonest dealings affect them and everyone around them.

Take Your Children to Work

When you take your children to work—either regularly or as a very special treat—they get to see where you go every day, and they get to see your values translated into real life.

At work, your children will hear your words of truth and see your acts of honesty. They will observe the difficult and challenging situations you face and watch you make your choice to do what is right.

In the "living laboratory" of your office, your factory, your plant, your lab, your classroom, your boardroom, your vehicle, your station-house, your theater, your fields, your ballpark, your arena—wherever you work—your children will see you put theory into practice and learn the real meaning of speaking the truth and dealing honestly.

There was once a king who invited his subjects to a royal banquet.

The king told each guest to bring a flask of wine, explaining that all the flasks would be poured into one large wine vat, from which the banquet's beverages would be drawn.

One of the king's subjects thought, "What will my small flask of wine mean? Instead of bringing wine, I will bring a flask of water. When my flask of water is added to all the wine, it will blend right in, and no one will know the difference."

On the night of the banquet, all the king's subjects assembled around the food-laden tables. The king welcomed his guests, and, then, summoned his servants to serve the wine from the one large vat.

The glasses were all filled—with water. For every one of the king's subjects had brought water, not wine, reasoning that one little flask of water would blend right in with all the wine, and no one would know the difference.

One dishonest act has the ability to produce far-rippling and far-lasting consequences; to bring ruin not only to the perpetrator but to everyone whose life is touched and affected; even, to shatter the entire social order.

As the maxim teaches, "Complete honesty, even in little things, is not a little thing at all."

Everywhere; All the Time

Honesty knows no season or locale.

You teach your children what it means to be an ethical person when you show them—in word and in deed—that truth and honesty are to be practiced every moment of every day.

In every instant—because the conduct of an instant has the power to change everything—each person can ask, "Am I doing right?" And—in the same instant—each person has the ability to change and do right.

The story is told that President Abraham Lincoln once signed an order transferring a certain army regiment from one assignment to another.

But the Secretary of War, Edwin Stanton, convinced that Lincoln had made a serious error of judgment, refused to carry out the order. Stanton was even heard to say, "Lincoln is a fool."

When Lincoln was told of Stanton's conduct—and his comment—Lincoln said, "If Stanton says I am a fool, then I must be a fool. For Stanton is almost always right. I think that I will go over to the Department of War and see for myself."

That is exactly what Lincoln did. Stanton was able to convince him that the order was a mistake, and Lincoln promptly withdrew it.

You can teach your children that moral strength lies not only in good and right judgment, but in the ability to listen and to

Return Library Books

Library books belong to the entire community.

When you return a borrowed book on time, you make it available for the other members of the community to enjoy, just as you did.

But, more importantly, when your children see you meeting the deadline for the loan, they will learn to follow the rules of the community, to respect the property—and needs—of others, to meet their obligations, to keep their promises, and to be fully honest in all their dealings.

learn; in the ability to be self-critical; and in the ability to recognize error and correct it.

You can teach your children that moral sense lies in affirming principle and maintaining integrity, while, at the same time, being open to new wisdom and new interpretation.

You can teach your children that moral greatness lies in being able to discern between the subtly conflicting claims of right and wrong, and in having the courage to say "yes" or "no" and mean it.

You can teach your children the ultimate definition of morality, of truth and honesty: "Wrong is wrong, even if everyone is doing it. Right is right, even though no one does it."

Evolving Consciousness

As with all great human endeavors—especially parenting—you will probably learn as much as you teach.

In teaching your children that truth and honesty are universal and eternal, you will, at the same time, learn from them

Check Your Check

When your restaurant check comes, check it to make sure that it is correct. Were you charged for anything you did not eat? Did you eat something for which you were not charged? Are the prices correctly added?

If something is incorrect, tell the wait person and ask to have it corrected—whether it is to your advantage or the restaurant's.

This is one of those times when "no one would ever know the difference," when you could "get away" without paying for dessert or coffee or a soft drink without anyone—except you—knowing.

But, the few seconds you spend checking for accuracy, and the honesty you display, even if—especially if—the mistake means that you will pay more money, will say more to your children about honest dealings than all the words you could ever speak.

that, just as surely, truth is ever-emerging and honesty is ever-evolving.

Your children will teach you that sometimes truth seems to depend on perspective.

A man saw a hippie riding on a bus, wearing only one shoe.

He said, "I see that you have lost a shoe."

The hippie replied, "No, man. I found one."

Your children will teach you that sometimes honest behavior seems to be affected by time and circumstance.

Stealing a horse is wrong.

Yet, over the years, in most places, the penalty for horse thievery has been reduced. Even though the act, itself, remains morally wrong, since horses are no longer as vital to a community's economic well-being as they once were, the consequences that society assigns to stealing a horse are no longer as great.

In the words of the modern essayist Ahad Ha'am, "Every generation has it own needs and its own truths."

So, part of teaching your children—even as you teach the great moral mandate of honesty and integrity—is understanding and heeding the advice of the sage who taught, "Do not limit a child to your own learning, for he was born in another time."

If you worry that evolving definitions of truth and honesty may confuse—and defeat—your desire for complete integrity, test yourself and your children by asking yourself and them if your conduct can hold up to the examination of public scrutiny.

It is told: twenty monks and one nun were learning meditation from a Zen master.

Even though her head was shaved and she wore plain clothes, it was evident that the nun was very pretty.

Several of the monks fell secretly in love with her, even though such a thing was clearly forbidden. One even wrote her a letter, professing his love and insisting on meeting her in private.

The nun did not reply to the letter. But on the following day, just after the master had finished his teaching, she arose before the group of monks.

Speaking to the one who had written her the letter, she said, "If you really love me so much, come embrace me now."

As parents and children, as human beings committed to lives of decency—as you seek truth and pursue honesty—together, through your ever-developing experience, you can come to share in the sentiments of Simone de Beauvoir, who said, "I tore myself away from the safe comfort of certainties through my love for truth. And truth rewarded me."

A Story to Tell Your Children

The Collector

The master and his assistant came to visit a rich man at his house. They came to ask him for money to help a man who was very sick.

The host greeted his guests warmly and listened carefully as the master told about the sick man and his needs. "We are asking you," said the master, "for a generous gift to help this poor man in his time of need."

The host asked, "Who is the sick man?"

The master shook his head. "You know that we cannot reveal the name of a person in need. In this case, it is very difficult for this man to admit that he is in need of charity."

"If I am to help, I insist on knowing the name of the man in need," said the host. "I promise that I will not tell anyone else. I was going to give you five hundred dollars. But, if you tell me the name of the man, I will give you one thousand dollars."

The master said, "I am sorry, but I cannot reveal the man's name."

"Two thousand dollars," said the host. "I will give you *two* thousand dollars if you tell me the man's name. Surely, you cannot refuse."

"No," said the master. "I will not break my word of honor to the man in need. I will not tell you his name, even for two thousand dollars."

"Three thousand dollars, then," said the host. "I will give you *three* thousand dollars to help the man if you will only tell me his name."

Before the master could reply, his assistant said to him, "Master, three thousand dollars will pay for all the hospital costs and all the living expenses. We cannot turn down our host's offer. He is an honorable man. I am sure that he will keep the secret. Just think how much good his money will do."

The master, again, shook his head, and walked toward the door, but he turned back to his host for a moment and said, "I should have left long ago. The honor of a man cannot be bought for any price. I will not reveal the man's name, and if that is the only way you will help him, then we will have to do without your help. I have other visits to make. Good day."

But before he could leave the house, his host begged the master to meet with him privately in the next room. The moment they were alone, the host broke into tears.

"Master," he said, "not long ago, I lost every penny I have ever saved. I cannot make the payments on my house; I have no money for food. I wanted to go to someone for help, but I could not stand the thought that everyone in the city would know that I need charity."

"Now I understand," said the master. "You were testing me to see if I could be trusted with your secret. Now that I know your need, I will ask for money for *you,* as well as for the man who is sick. Do not worry. Your secret is safe with me."

Their private meeting finished, the master and his host returned to the room where the assistant was waiting. With a fond good-bye, the master and his assistant left their host's home, and walked toward the place of their next visit.

"Well," asked the assistant, "how much did he give you?"

The master smiled, and, then, playfully shook his finger at his assistant. "Shame on you. You know that those things are a secret."

Questions to Discuss with
Your Children About Honesty

A Question to Discuss with Your Children (Ages 4–8)

Your teacher asks who spilled juice during snack time. You did.

Do you tell?

A Question to Discuss with Your Youngsters (Ages 9–12)

You find five dollars on the sidewalk near school.

What do you do with the money?

A Question to Discuss with Your Teenagers

Your friend got a copy of the answers to the questions on tomorrow's math test and offers to give them to you.

Do you take them? Why? Why not? What do you say to your friend?

A Prayer About
Being Honest

May the words of my mouth,
and the work of my hands
always be acceptable to you, Oh God;

so that all that I say,
and all that I do,
will bring honor to my life,
and glory to Your great and holy name.

Amen.

Traditional Hebrew prayer
adapted by Morris Silverman, Ben Saul, and W. D.

―――――――――⟨∞⟩―――――――――

*"Justice, Justice Shall
You Pursue"*

The Ethic of
FAIRNESS

*A wise old judge was once asked to settle a dispute between
two brothers over the fair division of a large estate that had
been left to them by their father.*

*The judge decided: "Let one brother divide the estate,
and let the other brother have first choice."*

*On a much smaller scale, my mother used the same sys-
tem to mediate between my sister and me when we were
growing up.*

*She called it her "candy bar" rule. If we were fighting
over the portion of a candy bar we were each to receive, my
mother declared: one of us got to cut the candy bar in half.
The other got to choose which half to take.*

Fair Fare

By the time they are two or three years old, children react when
they feel that their boundaries, their rights, and their sense of fairness and justice are being violated.

At home, on the playground, or in school, children are often heard crying out, "It's not fair!"

Naturally protective of their own rights, children can learn to extend the same moral imperatives to others.

You can teach your children that an ethical person does what is right and fair and just.

Yet, a modern parent's job is not as easy as it sounds—or as it once was.

In a society that has so many different definitions, so many competing interests, so many opposing claims—when even the courts are clogged with combative litigants demanding their own versions of truth and justice—how are you and your children to know what is just, what is fair, what is right?

To help them—and you—decide, tell them this story.

A young man knocked on the door of a woman's house and asked her if she would like to buy some of the delicious strawberries he had just picked from his father's fields.

"Yes," said the woman. "I would very much like to buy your fresh berries. I'll just take your basket inside the house and measure out two quarts."

The boy stood on the porch and began to play with the woman's dog. "Wouldn't you like to come in, and see that I measure the strawberries correctly?" asked the woman. "How do you know that I won't cheat you, and take more than two quarts?"

The young man replied, "I am not afraid, for you would get the worst of the deal."

"Get the worst of the deal?" the woman said. "How could that be? What do you mean by that?"

And the young man said, "Why, ma'am, if you take more than the two quarts of strawberries that you are paying me for, I would only lose the berries. You would make yourself a liar and a thief."

As the old Russian proverb teaches, "With justice, you can make a tour around the world. With injustice, you cannot even cross the threshold."

```
┌─────────────────────────────────────────────────┐
│              ┌─────────────────┐                  │
│              │   LUMIE 11      │                  │
│              └─────────────────┘                  │
│                                                    │
│            **Play Board Games**                    │
│                                                    │
│   Popular games like checkers, chess, Monopoly,    │
│   Scrabble, and many other board games can be      │
│   used to teach your children specific skills,     │
│   but, more importantly, they can be used to con-  │
│   vey your basic values.                           │
│                                                    │
│   When you play board games with your children,    │
│   you give them the gift of your time, and you     │
│   have a nonthreatening, playful way to show them  │
│   how to be honest and how to play fair—very       │
│   valuable lessons in the "game of life."          │
│                                                    │
└─────────────────────────────────────────────────┘
```

Justice for All

You can teach your children that an ethical person fiercely champions justice and equality for every human being—even if it brings personal conflict or pain.

When I was in Little League, my league could not afford to pay professional umpires, so the fathers of the players took turns umpiring the games.

The unwritten agreement was that no father would ump at his own son's game. But every once in a while, the schedule inadvertently put father and son together on the same field.

On the day that I saw my father standing behind home plate ready to officiate at my team's game, I was, at first, embarrassed—wouldn't that be the reaction of any twelve-year-old kid?—and then, strangely confident. "Hey," I said to my teammates, "we've got it made. My father won't want us to lose. He knows how much this game means to me."

Somewhere in the back of my mind, I remembered that my Hebrew school teacher had taught us that when the line from the prayerbook says that "your Father is your judge," it means that he will treat you with gentle kindness and mercy.

I had forgotten that my Hebrew school teacher had *also* said that the same line also means that when "your Father is your judge," he will judge with absolutely impartiality, lest he be accused of bias or favoritism.

And, most of all, I had conveniently forgotten what an honest man my father is.

I struck out only twice that entire Little League season—once in the very first game in my very first time up at bat and once when my own father called me out on strikes on a pitch that, to this day, I swear was at my shoe tops.

"How could you do that to me?" I cried at home that night. "You humiliated me in front of my whole team, in front of the whole league. And it wasn't even a good pitch. It was low—far too low to be called a strike."

In reply, my father told me this story.

There was a judge in a small town—where there was only one other judge serving the entire court system—who was widely respected for his fair and impartial decisions.

One day, the judge's wife raised an outcry because she believed that her maid—a poor orphan girl—had stolen a very valuable object from the family home.

The frightened servant vehemently denied the accusation, but the judge's wife said, "We will let the courts settle this matter."

When the judge heard his wife's plan, he immediately put on his best suit.

"Why are you putting on your good suit?" asked his wife. "You know it would be improper for you to accompany me to court. I can certainly plead my own case."

"I am sure you can," replied the judge. "But, who will plead the case of your maid, the poor orphan? I am going to court to see that full justice is done."

It is not always easy to be fair and to play fair, to be just and to do justice—especially when there is so much at stake, especially when friends and associates, or even your children, may be hurt. But, being fair and acting justly are the marks of an ethical person.

Don't Yell at the Umpire

When you attend a sports event—particularly a game in which your children are playing—try your best—even though it will, sometimes, be very, very hard—not to yell at the umpire or referee.

It can't be easy to be out there, continually making split-second decisions in the glare of public scrutiny. It can't be easy knowing that, at any moment, at least half of the players, and, perhaps, all of the fans in the stands may become angry and abusive. It takes a real sense of self, and a true commitment to impartiality and fairness, in order to be an umpire.

When you control your feelings, you teach your children both respect for authority and respect for the individual human being who is umpiring. You teach your children restraint and self-control; you teach them the good will and decency that will reflect in every place in their lives.

Equality for All

You can teach your children that acting justly means more than doing what is right and fair. Actively pursuing justice means working to right the wrongs, to balance the indignities, to fight for the good causes, and to bring human dignity into this well-intentioned but imperfect world.

When you can teach your children that **an ethical person knows that all people are created equal, that each human being has infinite worth,** they will not make a mistake like this:

The priest of a fashionable parish arranged to have the ushers greet people after the Sunday service.

The bishop finally persuaded the priest to greet each worshipper himself by saying, "Aren't you concerned that you do not know some of the members of your own congregation?"

The very next Sunday, following the service, the priest, himself, stood at the door of the church. The first person to leave the sanctuary was a woman plainly dressed, seeming to be somewhat out of place in the neighborhood.

"How do you do?" said the priest. "Welcome. We are very glad to have you with us here today."

"Thank you," said the woman, rather puzzled.

"I hope that we will see you often at services. We are always glad to see new faces."

"Yes, sir."

"Do you live in this parish?"

The woman seemed at a loss for words.

"If you give me your address, I will be glad to call on you some evening," said the priest warmly.

"You won't have far to go, sir," the woman replied. "I'm your cook."

It was then that the priest felt the power of the prayer—which can be your children's prayer, too—"Lord, open my eyes, that I may truly see."

Overcoming Prejudice

You can teach your children that an ethical person demonstrates commitment to justice and equality by not being influenced by preconceived ideas, but by judging each situation by its circumstances and each person by his or her own merit.

Your children do not want to be like the group of tourists who were stranded somewhere in the countryside when their bus broke down.

To alleviate their hunger, they were given old army rations to eat. But before eating the food, they tested it by throwing it to a dog who happened by. The dog seemed to enjoy the food and suffered no ill effects, so the tourists ate the rations.

The next day, the tourists learned that the dog had died. Everyone was panic stricken. Many complained of nausea and fever, and some began to vomit. A doctor was quickly called to treat the victims for food poisoning.

The doctor began his examination by asking about the dog. Did anyone know what had happened to the dog that died?

"Sure," said a neighbor. "The dog landed in a ditch, after it was run over and killed by a passing car."

The bus tourists learned what your children can come to know: the longest leap in the world is the jump to a conclusion.

You can teach your children that an ethical person demonstrates a commitment to human equality and decency by not displaying ignorance or prejudice.

Your children do not want to be like the sophisticated city dweller who was sitting in the lobby of a fancy hotel.

Sitting next to him was a Native American—a chief in full ceremonial dress.

The city dweller stared at the chief for a long moment, and then could no longer restrain his curiosity. "Excuse me," he said. "I can't help but notice your costume. Are you really a full-blooded Native American?"

"Well, no," replied the chief thoughtfully. "I am short one pint that I gave to save a white man's life."

The city dweller learned what your children can learn: that ignorance and prejudice are not the problems. It is not knowing that we are ignorant or prejudiced that causes difficulties.

Looking Closely

You can teach your children that an ethical person demonstrates commitment to justice and equality by not judging people by outward appearances.

An elderly couple was introduced to Charles Eliot, the president of Harvard College.

They said, "We wish to know more about your college because we are considering making a contribution in memory of our son who was killed in the war."

Eliot looked at the man and his wife, who were dressed in very plain clothes and seemed rather unworldly and unsophisticated. Instinctively, he felt that their contribution would not be very substantial, so he gave them only a few minutes of his time.

Sensing that they had been rather rudely dismissed, the couple decided not to make a contribution to Harvard.

Instead, they took their money all the way across the country to a small town in northern California. There, they used their wealth to establish a university, which they named in memory of their beloved son.

To this day, Leland Stanford University is known as "the Harvard of the west."

As the old rabbinic adage teaches your children, "Do not look at the container. Rather, look at what is inside it."

As You Judge, So Shall You Be Judged

You can teach your children that an ethical person respects differences and tolerates disagreements, without making negative judgments or taking personal offense.

There was once a master who was greatly revered by people as a true man of God. Every day, there were crowds of people at his door, seeking advice, or healing, or the wise man's blessing. Each time the master spoke, people would absorb his every word.

There was, however, one man in town who always contradicted the master. He mocked the advice the master gave and made fun of the people who came for his counsel.

The master's disciples disliked this man intensely, for he was offensive and insulting toward their sage.

One day, without warning, this man died. Everyone heaved a private sigh of relief. While outwardly they looked appropriately solemn, inwardly their hearts were glad, for this negative spirit would no longer be around to criticize and mock their master.

So the people were genuinely surprised to see their master in deep grief at the funeral.

One of the disciples asked, "Master, are you mourning over the eternal fate of the dead man?"

"No," replied the master. "Why should I grieve for our friend who is already in heaven? I am grieving for *myself*.

"This man was the best friend I had. All day I am surrounded by people who revere me and accept my every word. He was the only one who ever challenged me. I fear that with him gone, I shall stop growing and learning."

And as he said these words, the master burst into tears.

The master understood the words of Jesus that your children can understand, too: "With the judgments you make, you will be judged, and the measure you give will be the measure you get."

The Honor of Another

You can teach your children that an ethical person never lets another be embarrassed or put to shame.

At the Sabbath meal, the disciples of Rabbi Zev Wolf always carried on their conversations in low and subdued voices, so as not to disturb the holy man who was deep in thought.

Now, it was the custom at Zev Wolf's house that anyone could come at any time, seat himself at the table, and partake of the Sabbath meal.

One day, a man whom the others knew as an ill-bred and ill-mannered person came to Rabbi Zev Wolf's table. As was the custom, room was made for him, and he was welcomed to the repast.

After a time, this man pulled a large radish from his pocket, cut it into a number of pieces, and began eating it—smacking his lips in obvious enjoyment.

Have a Pillow Fight

If board games are helpful in teaching your children how to play fair, a pillow fight with you is even better!

Pillow fights are not just for adolescent slumber parties. They are great for parents and children.

Your children will quickly learn the "rules of combat," and the boundaries of what is permissible and what is not. They will learn what is "fair," and what is a "foul." They will learn that having an "opponent" does not mean having an "enemy." They will learn to "do battle" for their cause and to respect the efforts of their "distinguished challengers." They will learn to play hard, but to be gentle enough not to hurt.

Let the feathers—or the foam rubber—fly, and let your children learn life's best—and, sometimes, hardest—lessons, right in their own beds.

The others at the table were unable to restrain their displeasure. "You glutton," they said to him. "How dare you offend this holy table with your bar-room manners?"

Though they kept their voices low, it was not long before Zev Wolf heard what was going on.

The rabbi looked up, and said, "You know, I really do not know why, but today I just feel like eating a delicious radish. I wonder whether anyone here could get me one."

Filled with joy and happiness, the radish eater ran up to the rabbi and offered him a piece of his radish, which Zev Wolf ate with great delight.

Rabbi Zev Wolf understood the teaching of the Talmud—which your children can understand, too—that "the person who shames another in public is as one who sheds blood."

Looking for the Good

You can teach your children that an ethical person overcomes personal antipathy, hostility, or hatred and looks for the good in all people.

The story is told of the patriarch Abraham, who invited a traveler into his tent for a meal.

As soon as the traveler learned of Abraham's devotion to God, he began to curse God and revile His name.

Livid with anger and indignation, Abraham banished the traveler from his tent.

When he was at his prayers that night, he said to God, "Today, I defended Your honor and Your glory by sending away a blasphemer who cursed You."

And God replied, "This man has cursed me for fifty years, and yet I have given him food every day. Couldn't you have put up with him for one meal?"

It's All in Their Minds

You can teach your children that an ethical person affirms justice and equality by opposing bias, bigotry, and discrimination—against race, religion, creed, gender, age—wherever and whenever they are found.

You can teach your children that all human beings are created in the image of God and have innate equality and inherent rights. You can teach your children that intolerance comes not from any outward reality, but from their own inner perceptions.

A farmer was working in a field when a stranger approached him. The traveler asked, "What kind of people live in the next town?"

The farmer replied with a question, "What kind of people live in the town you just left?"

"They were horrible," the traveler said. "They were dishonest and selfish and inconsiderate. I'm glad to be gone from them."

The farmer looked up and said, "I am sorry to say that's what you'll probably find in the next town too."

Later that same day, another traveler approached the same farmer. "What kind of people," the traveler asked, "live in the next town?"

Again, the farmer replied with the same question he had asked the first stranger, "What kind of people live in the town you just left?"

"Oh," said the traveler, "they were thoughtful and friendly and kind. I hated to leave them."

"Well," said the farmer, "I am pleased to say that's what you'll probably find about the folks in the next town too."

You can teach your children the old proverb that "thoughts become action; action becomes character; and character determines our destiny."

You Can Be the One

You can teach your children that an ethical person brings justice to the world by working for honorable causes and for people who need help.

No matter how overwhelming the task of championing justice seems, you can remind your children of the words of President John F. Kennedy, who said, "One person can make a difference, and every person should try."

You can tell them about Abraham Lincoln, who saved a nation, and about Mahatma Gandhi, who moved the world with moral persuasion. You can remind them about Rosa Parks, who refused to move to the back of the bus, and about the Rev. Dr. Martin Luther King Jr., who brought dignity to a people. You can tell them about Lech Walesa, a shipyard electrician who rose to be president of his country by standing up for human rights. And you can remind them about Nelson Mandela, jailed for decades for his opposition to his government's policies of segregation and discrimination, but who came out of his bondage to quietly, and nonviolently, overthrow the oppression, help end apartheid in South Africa, and become president of his nation.

Or you can tell them about Adam, the young son of my friends Steve and Barbara.

When Adam was nine years old, he attended a school that had a large grassy area on one side of the school building. It wasn't exactly a sports field, but, to youngsters, it was the perfect place for a game of football during recess. For weeks, the young students played their game until one day, a notice came from the principal's office. The playing of football was no longer permitted on the grassy area because, the principal announced, she was afraid that one of the children would run into the large, concrete light pole in the center of the field and get hurt.

Adam was angry! The recess football game was very important to him and his friends. No one had ever gotten hurt on the pole. He and his friends were smart enough to stay away from it. The principal wasn't being fair!

Adam went into action. He wrote a very clear description of the issue and the problem, and he had all his classmates sign a petition addressed to the principal and the members of the school committee asking that the students be permitted to continue their football game. He was invited to appear before the school committee, where he stated his case clearly and forcefully.

The principal and the members of the school committee were so impressed with Adam's petition and presentation that they voted to let the football game continue. To solve the problem of potential injury, the school committee also voted to buy protective padding to place around the pole!

While not (yet) at the magnitude of saving a nation or bringing equality to an entire race of people, young Adam has already demonstrated the devotion and the courage it takes to champion a cause and has proven that one person *can* make a difference.

And he already understands a maxim of the rabbinic sage that you can teach you children: when it comes to working for human

Turn Off the Television

Your children deserve a better view of life than most contemporary television programs convey.

Too many television shows debase and crush the human spirit and diminish human dignity, by depicting crime and violence, indecency, injustice, and inhumanity.

When you have the courage to say "no" and use your finger to turn off the television set, you are rescuing your children from the "vast wasteland," and you are giving them the gift of time and mind to use in much more productive ways.

---

justice and equality, "It is not your task to complete the work, but neither are you free to desist from it."

There is a whole world of injustice and broken dreams that needs your children. You can guide them toward fixing it, and they can keep trying and trying and trying.

Unity in Purpose

While as unique individuals, there are surely many things which make us different, as children of God, as children of the universe, there is far more that unites us.

Lest your children ever forget their singleness of purpose with every other human being on the face of this earth—and their ethical commitment to insist on justice and equality for all—you can tell them this story.

Two little girls—one Jewish and one Christian—were the best of friends.

After Christmas, the little Christian girl was asked by her grandfather what gifts her best friend had received for Christmas.

Turn On the Television

Despite its many shortcomings, television can be a wonderful and a powerful tool to open up new worlds to your children. If used correctly, television is, in the words of the late Edward R. Murrow, "an instrument which can teach, illuminate and inspire."

Through the miracle of modern technology, your children can visit places they might otherwise never see, learn from people they might otherwise never meet, and be exposed to ideas they might otherwise never hear.

From good television programs, your children can see humankind's greatest creative possibilities; civilization's highest achievements; and the human spirit elevated to its finest.

When you help your children choose television programs wisely and well, you help them see how much wider—and more noble—their world can be.

The girl replied, "She didn't get anything for Christmas. You see, I'm Christmas, and she's Chanukah. I'm Easter, and she's Passover."

Then, with a big smile, she added, "But we're both Thanksgiving."

The necessity of bringing justice into the contemporary world is well established.

As the late political activist Cesar Chavez taught, "It was all done by Christ and Gandhi and St. Francis of Assisi and Dr. King. They did it all. We don't have to think about new ideas."

And our task is clear.

For, Chavez added, "We just have to implement what they said, just get the work done."

To this call to action—to this challenge to make a better, more just and righteous world—all you and your children can add are the words spoken by the Children of Israel, as they were given the moral mandate at Sinai: "All that we have heard, we *will* do."

A Story to Tell Your Children

In Your Hands

In a faraway kingdom, a long, long time ago, the captain of the king's guard stopped a poor peasant in the street.

The peasant could see, by the gleam in the guard's eye, that he was in for some trouble.

The guard had his hands cupped, as if he were holding a precious thing that was twitching and turning and trying to escape.

"What do you think I have in my hands?" the guard asked the peasant.

The peasant was no fool, and, besides, he saw a tiny feather float out from between the guard's fingers.

"It is obvious," said the peasant. "You have a little bird cupped in your hands."

"Ah, you are right," said the guard. "But now, tell me. Is the bird dead or alive?

"Tell me the correct answer, and you may go on your way. But, tell me the wrong answer, and I shall put you into the king's jail, and you will stay there for many nights."

The peasant knew that he had a big problem.

If he said that the bird were dead, the guard would simply open his hands and let the bird fly away. But, if he said that the bird were alive, the guard could easily crush the little bird and kill it. Either way, the peasant would be wrong, and he would be headed for jail.

Faced with going to jail for either answer he gave, the peasant thought for a moment that he would say that the bird were dead. That way, the guard would open his hands, let the bird fly away, and, at least, the life of the bird would be saved.

But the peasant was smarter than that.

He knew that there had to be a way to be fair to the little bird—to make sure that the bird would not die unjustly—and, at the same time, to be fair to himself—to make sure that he would not go to jail unjustly.

So he said to the guard, "You ask whether the bird is alive or dead. The answer is in your hands. The answer is in *your* hands."

Questions to Discuss with Your Children About Being Fair

A Question to Discuss with Your Children (Ages 4–8)

When you are playing at recess, one of the kids keeps telling you that you aren't being fair because you take too long a turn on the swings.

What do you say? What do you do?

A Question to Discuss with Your Youngsters (Ages 9–12)

Twelve pencils are missing from the supply cabinet in your classroom. Your teacher says that unless someone confesses to taking the pencils, everyone in the class will be punished. You know who took the pencils.

What do you do?

A Question to Discuss with Your Teenagers

Your best friend cheated on the written exam portion of the driving test—but he didn't get caught, and he got his license. You are worried that his lack of knowledge of the rules of the road will endanger not only his safety, but the safety of others.

What do you do?

A Prayer for Justice

Oh, God, our Father and Mother,
who created us in a rainbow of colors,
hear us.

Teach our hearts
to protest against indecency
toward any of Your children;
and to demand justice and equality,
for all of Your children.

Deliver us from temptation and evil,
for Yours is the kingdom,
and the power,
and the glory,
for ever and ever.

Amen.

Inspired by Father Malcolm Boyd;
adapted by W. D.

The **4**TH

GOLDEN RULE

*"Do Not Separate Yourself
from the Community"*

The Ethic of
RESPONSIBILITY

*When I was growing up, almost every boy—and many
girls—in this country could name every player on his city's
baseball team.*

*We knew their positions, their places in the batting order,
their batting or earned run averages, their uniform numbers.
We knew their importance to the team, and, sometimes, we
even knew them personally, for during the winter, they would
attend programs at local churches, synagogues, and youth
centers to meet their fans and sign autographs.*

*Winning the pennant was everything. The team was
paramount. Everyone—players, managers, coaches, owners,
fans—worked and rooted toward the common goal. Victory
meant collective pride and celebration. Defeat meant bitter
disappointment.*

*I remember one weekend in the summer of 1959—the
highlight year of my childhood because that was when my
Chicago White Sox finally won the American League pennant—when the White Sox played the dreaded New York*

Yankees in a series that would have a great effect on the outcome of the pennant race. The entire city huddled around radios and hung on every pitch. When the White Sox swept the four games, there was city-wide euphoria.

The night the Sox clinched the pennant—frightening my grandmother, but delighting every baseball fan—the mayor set off the city's air-raid siren. We danced in the streets.

When a popular home-team player was traded to another team, it was a day of city-wide grief and mourning, for we all felt a real sense of loss that someone from our team—our family—was leaving us.

Then, in the early 1970s, Major League Baseball permitted limited "free agency," deciding that a player could sell his services to the team that bid the highest price. Those who rejoice that America was built through the strength of labor unions and the rights of individual workers hailed the decision. But, baseball was changed forever.

Now, players change teams as often as they change socks. They no longer seem to care about the good of the team, about the team winning, about the pride of the city. They care, instead, about their personal achievements and statistics, which will earn them more money from another team in another city as soon as they are eligible to be free agents.

Instead of being a team sport—with its participants working for the common good of the team—professional baseball has now become groups of loosely connected individuals, each working for his own personal good.

Our children are left bewildered and uncertain.

Their heroes leave them without warning. Their role models disappear on the wings of self-interest.

Whom can they count on anymore? Whom can they depend on anymore? Who will be there for them anymore?

As the song so poignantly asks, "Where have you gone, Joe DiMaggio?"

From "Us" to "Me"—and "Not Me"

In the 1950s, and into the early 1960s, much of the American agenda was centered around building up and maintaining communities—from the close-knit inner-city neighborhoods, to the GI housing projects, to the burgeoning suburbs.

America still sat on the front porch, knew the neighbors, and had block parties on the 4th of July.

But the 1960s brought upheaval and radical change.

No longer would the presumed authority of parents, teachers, or government go unchallenged. No longer would the past be the unquestioned blueprint of the future.

One generation toppled two presidents, stopped a war, and got civil and human rights for all citizens. The drug culture swept the campuses. Racial, political, sexual, and feminist revolutionaries took to the streets, and changed the face of America forever.

The causes were just, but the price was high.

Instead of being—even if only in theory—"one nation, under God, indivisible," America became a country where everybody was encouraged to "do your own thing."

The degree to which selflessness had given way to selfishness, community had given way to individualism, was vividly portrayed on posters that adorned hundreds of thousands of dorm rooms on college campuses across the country.

The words of the psychologist Fritz Perls admonished, "I do my thing and you do your thing. I am not in this world to live up to your expectations. And you are not in this world to live up to mine. You are you, and I am I. And if by chance we find each other, it is beautiful. If not, it can't be helped."

Who cared about commitment anymore? Who cared about obligation anymore? Who cared about responsibility anymore? Who cared about the common good anymore?

Taken further, who cared about teamwork anymore? Who cared about self-sacrifice anymore? Who cared about community anymore? Who cared about anyone or anything except *"me"* anymore?

America became fractured and fragmented. It soon became "every man, every woman, for him/herself."

The excesses of the 1960s led to the "ME Decade" of the 1970s, and the "Greed Decade" of the 1980s.

And now, we have become a nation that is defined not by its greater whole, but by its widest extremes—black and white, rich and poor, the powerful and the powerless.

We are a nation that can hardly pass a bill in Congress anymore without compromising principle to political expediency.

We are a nation with few articulated values and little clear direction, constantly in fear of being swamped by the wave of narrow self-interest and militant self-protection of "ME ism."

And we are, at the very same time, a nation beset by the plague of "NOT ME ism."

Time and time again, we see people unwilling to take responsibility for their actions, unwilling to accept the consequences of their conduct.

"I'm not guilty. It's not my fault," we hear over and over again. "I did it because (choose one or many) I was underprivileged; I was overindulged. I was discriminated against because of color, race, religion, ethnic background, gender, age. I was abused as a child; I was battered as an adult. I trusted someone else; I was never able to trust anyone. I was betrayed, duped, used by my mother, father, child, spouse, partner, doctor, lawyer, accountant, therapist, priest, minister, rabbi, the police, the government. Not me! I'm not responsible. I'm not the perpetrator. I am the victim."

The greater good has been crushed by self-serving selfishness and self-indulgence.

How can we hope that our children will feel any obligation to other human beings when we adults are so self-centered?

How can we expect our children to have any sense of communal responsibility when we adults are so self-seeking?

Back to You

You could despair that communal unity will never again be restored to America. But then, you would become part of the problem instead of part of the solution.

There was a woman who complained to her friend that her next door neighbor was a poor housekeeper.

"You should see how dirty her house is. It is almost a disgrace to be living in the same neighborhood. Just look at those clothes she has hung out on the line. Look at those black streaks on the sheets and the towels!"

The friend walked up to the window and said, "I think that the clothes are quite clean, my dear. The streaks are on your windows."

When your children see you participating in the community and working toward the common good, they will learn how to be active, involved members of the community.

Back to "Us"

In Africa, it is said that it takes an entire village to raise a child. And in China, when a patient is released from a mental hospital he is not sent off on his own. Rather, he is given over to the care of an entire committee of his family and friends who assume responsibility for his reintegration into society.

The poet John Donne rightly observed that "no man is an island." We human beings are most comfortable—and most successful—as part of a group, a tribe, a clan. We share wisdom, learning, experience, energy, strength. We are better for being with each other than in being alone.

Individual sticks are easily snapped. Held together, the singular sticks become part of a bundle that cannot be broken.

Vote

It may sound trite, but it is true: one of the greatest privileges you have, one of the greatest freedoms you possess, is your right to vote—to elect those who represent you in government, and to determine the policies by which you live.

Every time an election is held, you can go to your polling place and cast your ballot.

When you take your children with you to see you exercise your right to vote, you show them democracy in action, and—most importantly—you show them what it means to actively participate in the process of building up and caring for a community and a country.

You can teach your children a sense of responsibility when you care about and for the people whose lives touch yours, and when you build up and sustain relationships of mutual faith and trust.

As the great sage Rabbi Hillel taught, "If I am not for myself, who will be for me? But, if I am only for myself, what am I?"

Building Community

A world-famous conductor came to direct a concert with one of Europe's most prestigious symphony orchestras.

At the rehearsal the day before the performance, the conductor taught the members of the orchestra a new and innovative interpretation of the piece to be played. The brass section was to play louder and more forcefully than ever before. The percussion section was to beat out a hard and deep rhythm. The strings were to well up their sound.

Volunteer

You show your children what it means to be a caring, participating member of your community when you volunteer your
time and talent to the people, institutions, or organizations that
desperately need you.

When you reach beyond yourself to share yourself with another, you help a community fulfill its responsibility to itself; you
enrich the life of another; and you ennoble your own life beyond measure.

When your children see you giving the work of your hands and
the passions of your heart, they will learn what it means to need
and be needed, to care and to share, to feel obligation and
commitment, and to meet their responsibility to their brothers
and sisters in the human community.

During the rehearsal, the piccolo player could hardly hear her
own notes. She thought to herself, "Despite his great reputation,
this conductor doesn't know what he is doing. He is ruining this
fine piece of music. My normally strong notes are totally lost over
the loud, pounding sounds the rest of the orchestra is making."
Disgusted, she stopped playing her part.

In but seconds—ever attuned to the subtle nuances of the entire orchestra—the famous conductor cried out, "Stop. Stop playing now. Where is the piccolo? Where is the piccolo?"

There are some experiences in life that cannot take place
without the full and active participation—and the implied con-
sent—of every member of the community. Some of life's most significant, enduring, and sweetest moments find their purpose and
their meaning only in the midst of community.

Ask your children: what fun is it to have a birthday party if none of their friends can come? Ask your older children: what real value is there to a school graduation ceremony if there is no one there to say, "congratulations"? From the youngest of ages, your children need their own little community, in order to mark and celebrate the important occasions in their lives.

Every cultural, religious, and spiritual tradition has a ceremony to welcome new-born infants into the community and to bestow upon them their names—the identity by which they will be known.

First Holy Communions and *Bar* and *Bat Mitzvahs* are always held within the circle of community, for matters of faith are not just private, but are to be affirmed by the members of the faith community to which the young person publicly pledges allegiance.

Weddings are conducted in the presence of the community, as the young couple asks the people amongst whom they live to witness the public declaration and commitment of their private love.

When a precious life is over, it is the members of the community who bring their friend and companion to a final resting place in land sanctified and consecrated by the community, with rituals and words of tribute spoken by the community.

With mutual commitment comes the sacred space and the sacred words that turn private yearnings and personal hopes into shared responsibility and communal celebration.

Far from being an onus that brings burden or hardship, mutual responsibility is a precious covenant that brings satisfaction and joy.

You can teach your children that being part of a community, being committed to the good of the community, being equally responsible for the prosperity and success of the community, enriches and ennobles the life of each and every person in the community.

As one of philosophy's oldest questions profoundly asks, "What is the sound of one hand clapping?"

Being Community

Two friends were out on the lake in a rowboat. One took a small hand drill from his pocket, and began to drill a hole in the floor of the boat.

His friend was flabbergasted. "Are you crazy? What are you doing? You will make a hole in the bottom of the boat, the water will flood in, the boat will sink, and we will drown."

The man with the drill replied, "Don't worry. I'm just drilling the hole under *my* seat."

What the driller forgot, you can teach your children: **that all human beings are interconnected at the deepest level. What happens** to one, happens to all. When one person hurts, every person hurts. When one person prevails, every person prevails.

No greater testimonial to the interdependent connection of all human beings was ever given than by the German Protestant theologian Pastor Martin Niemoller.

Shortly after World War II—not long after his release from a Nazi concentration camp—he said, "In Germany, they first came for the communists, and I didn't speak up because I wasn't a communist. Then they came for the Jews, and I didn't speak up because I wasn't a Jew. Then they came for the trade unionists, and I didn't speak up because I wasn't a trade unionist. Then they came for the Catholics, and I didn't speak up because I wasn't a Catholic. Then they came for me. And by that time, there was no one left to speak up."

Similarly, the Zen koan teaches, "One day Chao-chou fell down in the snow and called out, 'Help me up! Help me up!' A monk came and lay down beside him. Chao-chou got up and went away."

You can teach your children: one drop of human evil poisons every human being. One moment of human decency ennobles every human being.

As the sages taught, "Every human being is responsible for—and is intimately affected by—the acts of every other."

And you can teach your children that their commitment and sense of responsibility to the community is, ultimately, their commitment and sense of responsibility to themselves.

The greater good is the good of each and every human being. Every individual act ripples deeply into the entire human community. Every communal act reflects back onto each individual.

A farmer, whose corn always took first prize at the state fair, always shared his best corn seeds with all the neighboring farmers.

When asked why, he said, "The wind picks up the pollen, and carries it from field to field. If my neighbors grow poor corn, the cross-pollination will bring down the quality of my corn. But, if

Visit a Sick Friend

It is not always easy, it is not always pleasant, to visit a friend who is sick—particularly one who is very ill. It can be frightening to see someone who is sick, and it can be confusing and even intimidating trying to say the right words and do the right thing.

When you take your children with you on a visit to the hospital bed or to the home of someone who is ill, you show them your caring and concern, and, more importantly, you show them your sense of responsibility to another human being who needs your presence and your help.

---

they plant the very best seeds, then *their* corn and *my* corn will always be of the most excellent quality. What is good for my neighbors is good for me."

You can teach your children: whatever you do for others, you do for yourself. What is good for them is good for you.

As the old proverb whimsically puts it, "We didn't all come over on the same ship, but we are all in the same boat."

All of Us

A woman who was celebrating her one hundredth birthday was being interviewed by the local newspaper reporter.

"To what do you attribute your longevity and good health?" she was asked.

"Well," replied the woman, "I never drank and I never smoked. I always got enough sleep, and whenever I felt ill, I went right to the doctor.

"I loved my husband and my children the best I knew how, and I love the Lord. I go to church every Sunday, you know.

Give Blood

With one of the simplest—and painless—acts of human kindness, you can connect with your fellow human beings at a deep and intimate level.

When you donate a pint of your blood to your local Blood Bank or hospital, you give the gift of hope and possibility, and, perhaps, even the gift of life.

When you take your children with you to watch you give your blood, they will learn that there are only two relevant questions: is your blood healthy, and are there those who need to receive transfusions of blood?

They will learn that the gender, race, religion, or creed of neither the donor nor the recipient is important. They will learn the unity—and the mutual responsibility—of all humankind.

"And," she added, almost as an afterthought, "I always tried to keep busy and do whatever I could to help out—as I do with Miss Sadie."

"Miss Sadie?" inquired the reporter. "Who is she?"

"Oh," said the woman, "she's the lovely little woman down the street. She'll be eighty-eight next week, but, poor thing, she broke her hip last month. So I go down to her house every day just to check up on her. Why just yesterday, I brought her some of my nice home-made biscuits. What a dear one she is."

You can teach your children the benefits of cooperation instead of selfishness, the blessings of community instead of self-interest, when you teach them not to build walls, but to build bridges; not just to pluck fruit, but to plant trees.

You can teach your children to know their obligation to their community—and the life-sustaining sense of satisfaction that comes with it—by remembering how a one-hundred-year-old woman still bakes biscuits for her eighty-eight-year-old neighbor.

And you can teach your children to feel their responsibility to every other human being by telling them these words from the *Upanishads,* "As is the atom, so is the universe."

And you can ask your children to take their rightful—and necessary—place in shaping and forging the human community by giving them the gift of this piece of old wisdom: "Coming together is a beginning; keeping together is progress; working together is success."

A Story to Tell Your Children

Stone Soup

A soldier rode his tired horse down a back county road, heading home from a lost battle. It was late afternoon, and he was very hungry.

Up ahead, he saw a small village and thought to himself, "I'll get something to eat there, and find a place to spend the night."

Suddenly, his horse tripped, throwing the soldier to the ground. As he brushed himself off, he saw that the horse had stumbled over a rock sticking up out of the middle of the road. With his sword, the soldier dug up the rock and saw that it was a beautiful stone—round and almost perfectly smooth. Instead of casting it aside, the soldier put the fine rock into his saddle bag, mounted his horse, and continued on his way.

As he approached the village, people stopped their work to stare. He waved to several of the townspeople, but no one waved back. At the first house, he saw a woman standing in the doorway. "Good evening," said the soldier. "I am wondering if you could spare a bit of food for a hungry man."

The woman shook her head, and said, "I am sorry, but there is barely enough food for our family."

The soldier continued on his way. He saw a man leaning against a fence. "Do you have a place at your table for a hungry soldier?" he asked.

"We've had no rain for a long time," the man replied. "The poor harvest left us with very little to feed our children."

At house after house, the soldier heard the same reply. "We are sorry, but we cannot invite you to eat with us. We hardly have enough food to feed ourselves."

Discouraged—and very hungry—the soldier sat under a tree and thought to himself, In a few weeks, these poor people will be as hungry as I am. There must be a way for them to find food.

Suddenly, he had an idea. He reached into his saddle bag, took out the rock, and called out, "Ladies and gentlemen, you are lucky that I have come to your village today. I have in my hands this special stone that will help you get through the long winter. If someone will get me a large kettle, I will boil some water, and make you a delicious stone soup!"

In just a few minutes, someone brought a kettle. The soldier filled it with water and started a fire underneath it. As soon as the water came to a boil, the soldier dropped the stone into the kettle. It wasn't long before he tasted the soup. "Delicious!" he exclaimed. "All it needs is a little salt and pepper."

"I have some salt and pepper," said one of the townswomen, and she ran off to get it.

A few minutes later, the soldier tasted the soup again. "Delicious!" he exclaimed again. "All it needs is some potatoes."

"I have a few potatoes in my kitchen," said another one of the townswomen, and she ran off to get them.

A few minutes later, the soldier tasted the soup once again. "Delicious!" he cried out. "All it needs is a carrot or two."

"I have a small bunch of carrots," said one of the townsmen, and he ran off to get it.

A few minutes later, the soldier tasted the soup yet again. "Delicious!" he said. "All it needs is a few leaves of cabbage."

"I have a cabbage," said a farmer, and he ran off to get it.

A few minutes later, the soldier tasted the soup again. "Delicious!" he cried once more. "If only we had a small piece of meat, this soup would be a really tasty stew."

"I have a piece of meat that I have been saving," said another one of the townswomen, and she ran off to get it.

By the time the soup was ready, it was almost dark. The men brought large tables and chairs; the women brought bowls and spoons. Soon, everyone was eating the stone soup. It was the most delicious soup anyone had ever tasted.

Everyone was smiling and laughing, and it wasn't long before a few of the folks brought out their fiddles and began to play. Everyone sang and danced until the wee hours of the morning.

The next day, as the soldier got ready to continue on his journey, the townspeople came to say good-bye. As he mounted his horse, he said, "Thank you for a very happy time. To show my appreciation, I am leaving the soup stone as a gift to you. You can use it to make stone soup any time you want."

And, from that day on, whenever they were hungry, the townspeople of that small village remembered the soldier and used the soup stone to make up another helping of the most delicious soup anyone had ever tasted.

Questions to Discuss with
Your Children About Responsibility

A Question to Discuss with Your Children (Ages 4–8)

Your best friend doesn't invite you to her birthday party.

How do you feel? What do you say to your friend?

A Question to Discuss with Your Youngsters (Ages 8–12)

One of the kids in your class has to stay home from school for two weeks because he broke his leg. Even though you aren't really friendly with him, he lives in your neighborhood. Your teacher asks you to bring him homework and explain the assignments to him—every day for two weeks.

Do you agree to do it? Why? Why not?

A Question to Discuss with Your Teenagers

Members of a secret gang are terrorizing some of the younger kids at school—especially with threats of physical violence and the demand for payment of "protection money." The kids who are threatened are really afraid and will not reveal the identity of the gang members.

The school principal asks you and five of your friends to see if you can find out who the gang members are and to report their names to the authorities.

Do you accept the principal's request? Why? Why not?

A Prayer for
the Human Community

Oh, Lord,
Open our eyes,
that we may see You in our brothers and sisters.

Open our hearts
that we may love each other as You love us.

Renew in us Your spirit,
and make us one.

Amen.

Inspired by Mother Teresa;
adapted by W. D.

"*Let the Poor Be Members
of Your Household*"

The Ethic of
COMPASSION

*Irving Cramer, the Executive Director of MAZON: A Jewish
Response to Hunger—an organization that collects and dis-
tributes money to feed hungry people—tells this story:*

In a kindergarten classroom in northern Minnesota, the
teacher asked the children, "How many of you had breakfast
this morning?"

About half the students raised their hands.

The teacher then asked those who did not raise their
hands, "Why didn't you eat breakfast today?"

Some said that they got up too late and didn't have time
to eat. Some said that they weren't hungry this morning. A
few said that they didn't like any of the food that had been
served to them.

All of the little students gave an answer—except one
little boy.

"And why didn't you have breakfast this morning?" the
teacher asked him.

"Because," he replied, "it wasn't my turn."

"It wasn't your turn?" asked the teacher. "What does that mean?"

"Well," said the boy, "there are five kids in my family. But we don't have enough money to buy enough food so that everybody can eat breakfast every day. We take turns eating breakfast, and today, it wasn't my turn."

The Needing Need

The United States of America is one of the richest and most prosperous countries in the history of human civilization.

Yet, there are so many who are in need: the hungry, the homeless, the illiterate, the orphan, the mentally disturbed, the substance abuser, the addicted, the habitual criminal, the battered and the abused, the poor and the impoverished, the refugee, the critically ill, and the severely disabled.

We deliberately do not call them "the needy"—for that would demark and classify them, and, perhaps, condemn them to a perpetual state of being.

But, we—who are more fortunate and greatly blessed—know that these millions of our fellow human beings are, at this very moment, "in need," desperately "needing" understanding, care, and hope.

They need our help.

You can teach your children that a good, decent, ethical person hears another's cries of anguish, and responds.

Your Money and Your Life

No matter how much money you have earned or accumulated, it is *only* money—paper or metal or electronic credits that sit in your mental counting house.

Money is worthless until it is used.

A miser hid his gold at the foot of a tree in his garden. Every week, he would dig up his treasure and stare at it for hours.

Fast

When you voluntarily refrain from eating one day a week—or one meal a day, or one meal a week—in some small way, you begin to understand the agony of those who refrain from eating day after day—not by choice, but because they have no choice.

For a few hours, you—and your children who fast with you—can feel the emptiness that the hungry feel every hour. You can know what it is to fear from want and to fear from need.

When you follow the old Native American adage of "walking in another's moccasins for a day," you can know how much hunger—and, by extension, so many other social ills—hurts, and you can choose to help alleviate human pain and suffering wherever it is found.

One day, a thief stole all the gold. When the miser came to look at his hoard, all he found was an empty hole.

The man began to cry with grief, so his neighbors came to find out what was wrong. After hearing the man's sad tale, one of the neighbors asked, "Did you ever use any of the gold?"

"No," said the miser. "I only looked at it once a week."

"Well, then," said the neighbor, "for all the good your money did you, you might just as well come every week and stare at the hole."

Certainly, you will spend some of your money for life's necessities and amenities, and you may spend even more to indulge in some of the luxuries of modern life. You will want security and peace of mind for yourself and your family.

But some of your money is not yours to spend on yourself.

As strange as this may sound, some of your money does not belong to you.

Some of your bounty, some of your abundance, is given to you to give to those in need.

There will always be debate over how your money can do the most good.

Some argue for immediate relief—and that kind of assistance is surely needed, for an empty belly knows no politics and cannot wait for the results of another government study or commission report.

Yet the reality is, that if one hundred million dollars were made available tomorrow to feed the hungry, that money could provide only ten meals for every hungry person in America. One hundred million dollars means breakfast, lunch, and dinner on Monday, Tuesday, and Wednesday, and breakfast on Thursday. Then, the one hundred million dollars would be spent, and the hungry would be hungry again by lunch time.

So, others argue that money is better spent on research, advocacy, and educational programs—in the image of the popular axiom, not just giving people a fish to eat today, but teaching them how to fish so that they can eat forever.

With worthy arguments on both sides of the issue, and knowing that the answer probably lies somewhere in the middle, one thing is clear: much money is needed to confront and conquer the social ills that beset our society and our world.

You can teach your children that a good, decent, ethical person gives financial resources to needing people and causes.

From Your Heart and Your Hands

The danger in giving money to worthy people and causes is that you may be lulled into the trap that "checkbook charity" will suffice—that giving a big enough contribution will both solve the problem and fulfill your obligation.

You can teach your children that a good, decent, ethical person not only hears another's cries, but also feels another's pain, and responds.

Contribute

There are hundreds of organizations and institutions that serve the needing which ask for your financial support.

When your children see you giving of your resources by writing a check to the Heart Fund, the Cancer Society, AIDS research, the United Way, the Special Olympics, your local police and fire fighters assistance funds, your local food pantry or soup kitchen, and the many, many other good causes that you can support, they learn what it means to care and to share with those in need.

When you give, you show your children both the goodness of your heart and the right thing to do.

As the Sabbath was about to begin, the rabbi had not yet appeared at the synagogue. His followers and disciples were deeply worried and filled with anxiety. The rabbi had never before been late for worship at the start of the Sabbath. When the sun set, he was always at his place along the eastern wall, ready to greet the holy day.

His followers sent out a search party to look for their rabbi. Where could he be? He was not at his home; he was not seen anywhere along the path. He seemed to have just disappeared.

The search went on, but darkness fell. The holy Sabbath had begun, but the rabbi was still missing. He had failed to come to the Sabbath service for the first time in his life.

Forlorn and disconsolate, his followers slowly made their way back to the synagogue. On the way, they saw a faint light coming from one of the tiny houses set back far from the road. Curious, they approached the house.

Have a Family "Piggy Bank"

In addition to letting your children see *you* write checks to support worthy causes, you can encourage *them* to make contributions themselves.

You can have a family "piggy bank" that serves as a family "charity box," so that your children can join you in giving their pennies, dimes, and quarters to the needy.

Special, specific times can be set aside for putting coins into the charity box—perhaps at the beginning of your weekly Sabbath observance or at holiday time. Donations can also be made by anyone at anytime—especially in celebration of happy events or when receiving good news (or a good grade on a test).

Each time the family charity box is filled up, you can have a "family meeting" to decide where the funds will be donated. All the contributors—especially the children—can be urged to "nominate" worthy causes for your family's gift.

By enabling your children to give their "own" money to real people and causes, you show them *how* to care and share from their own hearts and their own pockets.

Looking through the window, they saw their rabbi sitting at the side of a bed, gently stroking the forehead of a feverish young boy.

Quietly, the rabbi's most learned disciple entered the house and approached his master.

"Rebbe, Rebbe," he said, "we were so worried. The Sabbath has begun, but you have not come to the synagogue. Rebbe, where have you been?"

And the rabbi looked at his disciple and said, "I have been right here, my son. You see, as I was walking to the synagogue,

I saw this frail young woman, this poor widow, out near the forest collecting a few sticks. I saw that the sticks were much too heavy for her to carry, so I offered to help her. It was then that she told me that her son is so very ill, and that she is without wood for the fire. So, I chopped some wood, and stoked the fire, and now I sit here with the boy—asking God to bless him and to heal him."

And the disciple understood that his rebbe was fulfilling God's law far more than by being in the synagogue for the beginning of the Sabbath. He was reaching out his heart and his hands to one of God's children who needed him. He was doing God's work on earth.

Hand to Hand

You can teach your children to give the work of their hands—even when it is not easy or pleasant.

Once a group of beggars afflicted with leprosy came to the Zen master Bankei, who was a great-hearted teacher.

Bankei welcomed the beggars, and he insisted on washing their bodies and shaving their heads with his own hands.

One of Bankei's devoted and prosperous supporters—a gentleman who had already built the master a temple in which he could train disciples and lecture to the people—witnessed the master tending to the lepers.

Revolted by the sight of the Zen master shaving the heads of the untouchables, the gentleman hurriedly brought a basin of water for Bankei to wash his hands.

But, the master refused, saying, "Your disgust is filthier than their sores."

The master knew that when you reach down into the mud to lift someone up, your hands may get dirty, but your heart remains clean.

"True Worth Is In Being"

You can teach your children that being able to give to others means—in modern parlance—understanding "where they're coming from."

As a woman approached her neighbor's home, she saw her friend's son mowing the lawn.

"Is your mother home?" she asked the boy.

He looked up from his work and replied, "You don't suppose that I'm cutting the grass just because it's too long, do you?"

Understanding and responding to the needs of others is not an inbred, human characteristic. It is an acquired trait that comes, first, with desire.

That is why King Solomon of old prayed, "Give Your servant an understanding heart. . . ."

Feeling another's pain as if it were your own, feeling true empathy and deep compassion, are not natural human instincts. They are attributes that are learned, absorbed, and ingrained by watching and listening and imitating.

Your children can learn to feel compassion when they see you caring deeply about other people; when they see your heart and soul powerfully touched by the plight of another; when they see you performing altruistic acts of loving kindness.

Seeing Faces

You can teach your children a life-long commitment to meeting the needs of others when you show them—by everyday example—a simple system of sharing and giving.

In *The Business Bible,* I told of how our family tried to put the ancient teaching of Rabbi Tanchum into modern practice. It is a lesson that is important for businesspeople to learn, but is even more imperative for parents and children.

Work in a Soup Kitchen

Your local soup kitchen, which feeds meals to hungry people, most likely depends on volunteers to staff the program.

Your children will see what it means to feel compassion and reach out with acts of loving kindness, to respond to the needs of others, when they see you give your time and your energy to do the necessary—and, sometimes, dirty—work that a soup kitchen requires.

When you give the love of your heart and the work of your hands to the needing, your children learn to have loving hearts and busy, helpful hands.

It is said of Rabbi Tanchum, "When he needed only one portion of meat for himself, he would buy two; one bunch of vegetables, he would buy two—one for himself and one for the poor."

When my sons were young, we put Rabbi Tanchum's custom into modern practice.

Every time we went to the supermarket, we would buy one extra item of nonperishable food—a box of cereal, a can of tuna fish, a package of macaroni and cheese, a jar of peanut butter.

We put the food directly into a brown paper grocery bag that we kept in the trunk of the car. When the bag was full, we delivered it to one of the food pantries or soup kitchens that helps feed hungry people.

It was really a very simple way of giving because it took no extra time or effort, and it cost only a few dollars a week.

How proud and happy Scott and Seth were when the bag in the trunk was filled up, and they could carry their groceries into the food pantry.

And what a powerful lesson it was! What a vivid, dramatic—and effective—way it was to teach young children the importance of giving and to infuse in them their personal responsibility to share—then and always.

And from the practice of buying one extra item of food for the hungry, *I* learned a great lesson that was taught to me by my son.

One day in the market, I took a box of Cheerios from the shelf and said, "How about these Cheerios as our food gift for today?"

Seth—who was about five or six at the time—grabbed the box of cereal out of my hand and said, "No!"

I watched him put the box of Cheerios back on the shelf, and, rather amazed, I asked, "Why not? Why shouldn't the Cheerios be our food gift for today?"

With righteous determination, Seth took a different box of cereal from the shelf, held it up to show me, and said, "Today we are getting Sugar Frosted Flakes because there are hungry kids out there too, and kids like Sugar Frosted Flakes better than Cheerios."

In an instant, Seth taught me to see the faces of the people we were feeding.

No longer could they be "the hungry," or "the needing," or "the people who come to the food pantry." They are people—with faces and names and stories. And I knew, from that moment on, that a person in need could never again be an anonymous number or statistic, but had to remain a human being, whose voice I can hear and whose hand I can hold.

When you teach your children to see the faces of the needing, you show them how to see both the beggar on the street and the lonely child on the playground, and you show them the way toward giving the gifts of decency and kindness, healing and hope.

As You Give

You can teach your children that as much as they give, they will receive much more—in joy, in satisfaction, in their own greater abundance.

Give Away a Pair of Socks

Many people give away old clothes to organizations like Goodwill or AmVets or the local housing shelter—which either give them to needing people, or sell them in a thrift shop, using the proceeds for further charitable work.

Most people give away an old suit, an old dress, a pair of pants, or an old sweater—items of clothing that may no longer be fashionable or may no longer fit.

The next time you and your children gather your old clothes to give away, in addition to your suits and dresses, give away a pair of socks—pieces of clothing that are always needed, but that few think to give.

And give a tube of toothpaste, a bar of soap, a bottle of shampoo, a roll of toilet paper, a package of disposable diapers—much needed everyday items that are often taken for granted unless you don't have them.

When you teach your children that giving is more than emptying closets of unwanted clothes, but is something that can be tailored to meet real human needs, you remind them to be thoughtful and respectful of the people who will receive their gifts, and grateful for the opportunity to share.

A modern master taught: "It takes courage to care; to fling open your heart and react with sympathy or compassion or indignation or enthusiasm when it is easier—and sometimes safer—not to get involved. But, people who take the risk, who deliberately discard the armor of indifference, make a tremendous discovery: the more things you care about, and the more intensely you care, the more alive you become."

The stories of two men teach the joy of giving.

When a friend asked Alexander the Great for ten coins, Alexander gave him fifty. When told that ten would be sufficient, Alexander replied, "True. Ten are sufficient for you to take. But not for me to give."

Nasrudin walked through the streets of his village saying, "My donkey is missing. Whoever returns the donkey will receive it as a gift."

The people could not understand what Nasrudin was saying. "You are making no sense. If the missing donkey is returned, why would you then give it away?"

And Nasrudin said, "If the donkey is returned, I will experience *two* of life's great pleasures: finding something that was lost, and giving away something of great value."

Simply put, you can teach your children the modern adage: "Give until it feels good."

So Shall You Reap

Measuring the depth of the human heart is no easy task.

There is no objective standard to tell you how much compassion and empathy your children feel, how passionately committed they are to alleviating human suffering. You can only hope that their conduct will manifest the values you have tried to convey.

I humbly tell you this next story not out of any sense of self-congratulations, and surely not to boast or brag, but to assure you that if you teach—and, most especially, model—over and over and over again, eventually your lessons will be internalized and your hopes for your children fulfilled.

If you haven't yet had this experience, you will one day learn that one of parenthood's most portentous moments is the day that you take your child to college to enroll in the freshman class.

Your "baby"—how could it possibly be eighteen years since he was born? Why I remember it as if it were yesterday—is about to go off on his own. There are still the tuition checks to write, and, hopefully, the advice to be asked. But, in the day-to-day of the everyday world, your child is grown up and gone.

If it is an intimidating and scary time for your child, it is—if absolute truth be admitted—an apprehensive and even traumatic moment for parents. (Just writing about the memory—even all these years later—is making my heart beat a little faster right now.)

You ask yourself: Did I do the best I could with this precious child? Was I a good enough parent? Did I pay enough attention to her? Did I give him enough time? Did I teach her all that I want her to know? Did I give him the tools to survive and flourish on his own? Will she make it? Will he be happy?

So, with a bit of false bravado from both parents and child, with emotions dancing just beneath the surface, and tears stinging just behind your eyes, you load the car with suitcases and sports equipment, the new word processor, and the old clock radio, and you head off to the big university.

We helped Seth carry all of his stuff up to his room. His mother made his bed. I tried to look busy arranging a few tapes and CDs on a shelf.

Then, it was time for lunch. The dorm cafeteria wasn't open yet, and the Student Union was jammed. So, we got in the car—inviting Seth's new roommate to join us—and headed for a local restaurant.

We parked at a meter on the street that took only quarters—at fifteen minutes of parking time per quarter—but among the four of us, we had only one quarter. So, as soon as we were seated in the restaurant, I handed Seth a dollar, and said, "Here, get four quarters from the cashier, and go out and put them in the meter."

A few minutes later, Seth returned, and I casually confirmed, "That gives us an hour on the meter, right?"

Seth replied, "Well, actually, we have only a little more than half an hour."

"How can that be?" I asked. "I gave you a dollar; that's four quarters. Four quarters buys us an hour of time."

And Seth said, "That's true but, as soon as I walked out of the restaurant, I saw a disheveled man sitting on the curb asking for spare change so that he could get something to eat. I gave him two of the quarters."

At that instant I knew that whatever my doubts and my fears about sending my son off to college, everything would be all right. He has the tools to endure, the values to prevail—to forge his place as a compassionate, caring human being.

What more could a parent ask?

There are so many people who need you and your children—to give sustenance and healing, encouragement and comfort, dignity and hope.

You can teach your children that a good, decent, ethical person has a big, loving heart when they feel you feeling another's pain, when they know that you are committed to alleviating human suffering, when they see the faces of the needing reflected in your face.

You can teach your children that a good, decent, ethical person has big, open hands when they watch you give of your resources—generously and often—and when they watch you give of the work of your hands—willingly and joyfully.

You can teach your children that a good, decent, ethical person can fulfill the sacred task of celebrating the spark of the Divine in each human being and the preciousness of each human soul when you teach them to imitate God who is "gracious, compassionate, and abundant in kindness; who forgives mistakes, and promises everlasting love."

A Story to Tell Your Children

Warm Fuzzies

Long, long ago, only very little people lived on the earth. Most of them dwelt in a tiny village, where they were very happy little people, with broad smiles and cheery greetings for everyone.

One of the things the little people liked to do most was to give Warm Fuzzies to each other.

Each little person carried a back-sack, which was filled with Warm Fuzzies. Whenever two little people would meet each other, they would give one another a Warm Fuzzy.

A Warm Fuzzy is a wonderful gift because it means, "You are special. I like you." So, the little people liked to give Warm Fuzzies because it made them feel good. And they liked to get Warm Fuzzies because the Warm Fuzzies made them feel very loved, and, besides, they were soft and cuddly against their cheeks.

The nicest thing about the Warm Fuzzies was that no matter how many a little person gave out, the Warm Fuzzy back-sack was always full. No one could ever run out of Warm Fuzzies.

Outside of the village, in a cold, dark cave, lived a great green troll. He really didn't like living by himself, but he couldn't get along with anybody else, and, besides, he hated giving or getting Warm Fuzzies. He thought Warm Fuzzies were silly!

One night, the troll was strolling in the village when he was met by a kindly little person.

"Here is a Warm Fuzzy for you," said the little person. "You don't come to town very often, so I am happy to see you, and I am very glad to give you a Warm Fuzzy."

The troll didn't want the silly Warm Fuzzy, and he was tired of hearing about Warm Fuzzies anyway, so he put his arm around the little person—as if he were telling a very special secret—and whispered, "You know, if you keep giving away all your Warm Fuzzies, one day, you will run out of them."

When the troll noticed the fear on the face of the little person, he looked inside his back-sack, and said, "Yep, I bet that you have only two hundred seventeen Warm Fuzzies left. You had better go easy on handing them out."

With that, the troll padded away, and a very confused and unhappy little person was left standing there.

Now, the troll knew that no one could ever run out of Warm Fuzzies. As soon as one is given away, another one magically appears to take its place. But, he wanted to see what would happen if he planted a tiny seed of doubt and worry in the minds of the little people.

Well, it didn't take long. The word soon spread. "If you give out too many Warm Fuzzies," the little people told each other, "pretty soon, you'll run out, and you won't have any more."

So, instead of giving each other Warm Fuzzies all the time—as they always had—the little people kept most of their Warm Fuzzies to themselves. Oh, every once in a while one little person would give a Warm Fuzzy to another, but it had to be a very, very special occasion—which didn't occur too often.

It wasn't long before the normally happy and cheery little people were feeling sad and gloomy. They no longer had the joy of giving away Warm Fuzzies, and they rarely felt the happiness of receiving one.

What was worse is that the little people began to distrust each other. They were worried that someone might steal some of their Warm Fuzzies. Soon, it wasn't even safe to be out on the streets after dark.

Most of the little people began to feel sick. They had pains in their shoulders and their backs because their back-sacks of Warm Fuzzies felt heavier and heavier to carry.

The troll was very pleased that his little lie had worked so well, but he was worried. "Gosh," the troll said to himself, "I just wanted the little people to see how silly Warm Fuzzies are. I didn't want them to be so unhappy, and I certainly didn't want them to get sick."

So the troll made up a plan. In his cave, he had a secret supply of Cold Pricklies. A Cold Prickly doesn't feel very good and isn't a very nice gift to give. But, since he had so many, and since the little people weren't giving away their Warm Fuzzies any more, the troll offered them a life-time supply of Cold Pricklies.

The little people were happy to have something to give each other again, but the trouble was that it just wasn't very much fun to give Cold Pricklies. No one knew what the Cold Pricklies meant, for, after all, they were cold and prickly. They didn't seem to mean anything about being special. They didn't seem to mean anything about friendship or happiness or love.

In the old days, when they got a Warm Fuzzy, most of the little people would say, "Wow!" Now, when they got a Cold Prickly, all they could say was, "Ugh!"

But, that's the way it went for a good long while. Most of the time, the little people gave each other Cold Pricklies, but every now and then—on a very special occasion—someone gave away a Warm Fuzzy. Then, everyone was very happy.

One day, one of the oldest and wisest of the little people said, "You know, things were much, much better here in our little village when we gave each other Warm Fuzzies. No one seems to like these Cold Pricklies very much, except for the troll. And really, no one likes the troll very much. You know, I think that it is time for us to give Warm Fuzzies again."

But most of the little people said, "Oh no, we can't do that. If we give away our Warm Fuzzies, we'll run out, and then we'll never have any more to give."

The wise one replied, "Our Warm Fuzzies aren't doing us any good now. They just stay in our back-sacks getting dusty. Keeping them to ourselves hasn't made us any happier. Let's try it again. Let's give our Warm Fuzzies to each other just like we used to, and let's see what happens."

And that is what the little people did. Soon, everyone was giving Warm Fuzzies to everyone else—just like in the old days. And guess what? Every time someone gave away a Warm Fuzzy from a back-sack, another one magically appeared. Once the Warm Fuzzies were shared again, there was a never-ending supply.

It wasn't long before the troll and his Cold Pricklies were completely forgotten, and all the little people of the little village gave their Warm Fuzzies to each other in love and with joy.

And happiness filled their lives once more.

Questions to Discuss with Your Children About Caring

A Question to Discuss with Your Children (Ages 4–8)

One of your friends never gets any dessert in his lunch box and always asks you to share your cookies.

What do you do?

A Question to Discuss with Your Youngsters (Ages 9–12)

Your youth group leader asks you not to go "trick or treating" this coming Halloween. Instead, you are asked to go from house to house asking for donations to help build the new youth center.

What do you do?

A Question to Discuss with Your Teenagers

A six-year-old child in your community was in a terrible car accident. The medical bills are much more than the family can afford. You don't know the child or the family, but the hospital announces that teenagers in the community can help pay off the bills by working at the hospital every Saturday or Sunday morning for the next two months—helping to clean up the grounds and weed the gardens. It will be hard, dirty work, and you must commit yourself for eight Saturdays or Sundays in a row—no absences are allowed.

Do you do it? Why? Why not?

A Prayer About Being Compassionate

Help us, Oh God,
to be like You.

As You are gracious and compassionate,
may we be gracious and compassionate.

Guide us and show us how to
feed the hungry,
and care for the sick;
to be eyes to the blind,
and feet to the lame.

Fill us with Your love,
so that we may do Your work
here on earth.

Amen.

Rabbi Jules Harlow, based on Jeremiah 9:22–23;
adapted by W. D.

The **6**TH

GOLDEN RULE

*"Consider the Marvelous
Works of God"*

The Ethic of
GRATITUDE

*Ever since the dawning of human history, human beings have
been fascinated with the vastness of the skies, the twinkling of
the stars, and, especially, the grandeur and the powerfully in-
tense attraction of the moon.*

*Finally, in this generation, humankind's ingenuity and
technological prowess made reality out of what had been only
a whimsical dream. A man walked on the moon.*

*One of the few astronauts to actually set foot on the moon
remembers what it was like to be there.*

*He looked out over the vast and majestic bleakness, the
stunning moonscape and the towering moon mountains.
Then, he looked back at earth—a huge blue ball, wrapped in
wispy clouds, gently floating in the blackness of the universe.*

*He was overwhelmed by the sheer beauty of the awesome
and magnificent sight before his eyes.*

*His thoughts, he said, went to the scripture he had
learned as a child, "How great are Your works, Oh Lord. In
Your wisdom, You created everything."*

But, in an instant, his mood was shattered, for he said to himself, "Stop wasting time. You're not here to be a tourist. Do your job. Go collect rocks."

Choices

In a world that is so utterly dominated by humankind's scientific and technological achievements, in a world where the genius of the human mind and the strength of human determination have accomplished so much, it is easy for human beings to become haughty and arrogant—to think that it is only our own capabilities and power that have gotten us what we have.

We might look at the universe and take it for granted, seeing it as formed through natural caprice and randomness, cleverly ordered and arranged by potent human hands.

But, the Bible warns, "You shall not say in your heart 'My power and the might of my hand have gotten me this wealth.' "

Then, and now, the wise teachings of scripture insist that human beings remember and revere the real source of all that we have, the ultimate—and only—source of our existence, our sustenance, our potential, our power, and our attainment.

You can teach your children that a good, decent, ethical person acknowledges and appreciates this great and glorious universe, rejoices in the miracles of the Creator, and celebrates the wonders of creation.

"The Answer, My Friend, Is Blowin' in the Wind"

You can show your children that the greatness of the universe is theirs to grasp.

You can stand with them in a cool lake, and let the gentle waves lap at your feet.

You can stand with them atop a majestic mountain, and let the wind blow through your hair.

Take a Walk

Take your children on a walk to show them the glories of the universe.

"Grass," said the poet, "is the handkerchief of the Lord." You and your children can experience the magnificence of the universe in every blade of grass and every flowering bud. You can come to know the greatness of the universe from towering trees and delicate ladybugs. You can see the whole universe played out in one tiny ant hill.

Whether you live surrounded by nature's beauty, or you must search for a sliver of blue sky peeking between city skyscrapers, you can show your children the wonders of their world and celebrate with them the splendor of creation.

You can lie with them on the ground, and let the earth's energy flow through you.

You can turn your faces to the sun, and let the glimmering rays bathe you in their golden warmth.

You can stand still with them, and let the awesome sounds of silence envelop you—interrupted only now and then by the song of a bird or the chirp of a cricket.

And, then, you can let your children—in their innocence and their eager intensity—remind you of some of the great pleasures of earthly existence: rolling in the ocean's waves; shouting at the top of your voice; laughing until your belly hurts; letting the juice of an orange roll down your chin.

The poet William Blake issued the challenge and the reward to you and your children: "To see a world in a grain of sand / And heaven in a wild flower / Hold infinity in the palm of your hand / And eternity in an hour."

Take a Hike

If a walk is good, a hike is even better. For on a hike, you can show your children the vast expanse of the universe.

On the heights of nature's summits and in the depths of her primordial beginnings, you and your children can be attuned to the rhythms of the cosmos and feel your place in the ongoing ebb and flow.

When you and your children have been deeply immersed in the grandeur of creation, then, with wholehearted admiration and gratitude, with great joy and deep humility, you can be moved to say, "Thank you."

The children of the universe can embrace the universe when you guide them toward its greatness—and theirs.

In Awe

It is no accident that the great cathedrals of medieval Europe are massive, striking structures.

They were purposefully designed, using sweeping architecture, to create a space that is awesome—that invokes the celestial heavens and transcends the place and the moment, transporting people from the here and now to thoughts and images of being in God's presence.

Government buildings were constructed in much the same way—as solid, substantial, grand edifices, built to inspire lofty thoughts and invoke high purpose.

In modern times—in our rush to be democratic and egalitarian and cost conscious—we have begun to construct religious and government buildings that are utilitarian and cost effective, but lack much awe-inspiring grandeur.

With little fashioned by human hands helping to sweep their eyes heavenward, children have few places to learn of awe and reverence.

Modern inventions occasionally astonish—how much more information can that tiny microchip possibly contain?—but advancing technology rapidly throws today's phenomenon onto tomorrow's ash heap of obsolescence.

So besides being immersed in the beauties and the wonders of the natural universe, your children have few places to be infused with a sense of transcendence, a sense of reverence and respect for things greater and grander than themselves.

It is told that when Lord Byron was a young student at Oxford University, he took an important examination in a religious studies course. The examination question was to write about the religious and spiritual meaning of the miracle of Jesus turning water into wine.

For three hours, Byron sat in the crowded classroom while all the other students busily wrote, filling up their examination books. But Byron sat, quietly pondering, not writing a word.

Finally, when the examination period was over, and all the other students had turned in their papers, the professor came to Lord Byron and said, "You cannot turn in a blank page. You must write something."

The young Byron finally picked up his pen, and wrote, "The water met its Master, and blushed."

That's awe!

That's reverence!

You can teach your children to feel deep respect and reverence, an abiding gratitude and overpowering awe in the presence of creation and the Creator.

Witness a Birth

There is no greater evidence of the majesty and the power of God than in the process of birth.

A miracle? Perhaps. But, more likely, a careful plan: oranges give birth to oranges, elephants give birth to elephants, elm trees give birth to elm trees, and human beings give birth to human beings—carefully designed with fingers, toes, and belly buttons, and the distinctly human ability to think and reason and remember; to hate and to love, to demand justice and feel compassion.

When you arrange for your children to witness a birth—a calf in the barnyard, a puppy or a kitten at home, a bird hatching from an egg, even a seed planted in a windowsill flowerpot—you let them experience and feel the awe of creation.

When you help your children sense the presence of God and the grandeur of the moment, you help them understand that as your children—and God's—they are precious parts of the intricate universe, unfolding just as it should.

". . . But the Earth Has Been Given to Humankind"

The heavens may be the dwelling place of God, but the earth has been given to humankind.

We are the stewards and the caretakers of the planet, responsible for preserving and protecting the beauty and the delicate balance of the place where we live.

The Navajo chant makes us aware: "I have been to the end of the earth. I have been to the end of the waters. I have been to the end of the sky. I have been to the end of the mountains. I have found none that are not my friends."

Yet, the pure, pristine garden that has been given to us as our home is increasingly despoiled by the work of our own hands. We pollute the rivers and choke the skies, strip the land and cut the forests bare.

We have not learned the simple truth that those native to America kept as their canon of faith: "The frog does not drink up the pond in which he lives."

Some have begun to understand. A nationwide chain of business service and copying stores determined that it takes one tree to supply 23,000 sheets of paper. So, for every 23,000 pieces of paper that the company sells, it plants one tree. In this ultimate recycling program, what is taken is returned, and the earth maintains its fragile equilibrium.

You can teach your children that a good, decent, ethical person works to preserve and protect the environment, and to bring healing, hope, and honor to our troubled and battered planet.

But there is more.

We can no longer go on thinking about the earth and the people who inhabit the earth as separate entities, as disconnected elements.

Chief Seattle taught, "All things are connected. Whatever befalls the earth befalls the sons of earth. Man . . . is merely a strand in the web of life. Whatever he does to the strand, he does to himself."

It is, perhaps, no accident that our universe has been recently beset by unusually numerous and fierce floods, earthquakes, and hurricanes.

How much blood of warfare can the earth soak up, how many vibrations of hatred can the earth absorb, how much pain can the earth take, before she reacts with trembling and upheaval?

In her pain, the earth is crying out: "Stop pounding me with your huge footsteps of riot and rebellion. Stop drenching me with the blood of your wars. For your pain becomes my pain. And you have put me in the kind of agony that causes my ground to rumble, my harsh winds to blow, my waters to deluge the lands."

In our highly intellectual rationalism—or in our arrogant self-centered selfishness—we have forgotten what our ancient ancestors knew well, and what those native to the land live out every day.

We and the earth on which we live are interlinked and interdependent at the deepest level.

And there is an intimate connection between human conduct and the favors or the alienation that the earth provides.

The contemporary spiritual guide Ram Dass put it this way: "In the ultimate depth of being, we find ourselves no longer separate, but part of the unity of the universe. That unity includes the sufferer and the suffering, the healer and that which heals. Therefore, all acts of healing are ultimately ourselves healing our Self."

You can teach your children that by respecting and redeeming their world, they are really saving themselves.

My friends Alan and Patty saw the powerful connection between the earth and its people when they recently took their sons on a family vacation.

Their older son, David, is a "typical" teenager. Like most teens, he is at the very center of his own world—the only world that seems to count to him. He is trying very hard to establish his own identity and to assert his independence by constantly playing to what the noted psychologist David Elkind calls the "imaginary audience"—the greater world he seeks to impress and influence.

His parents—like most parents of most teenagers—see his swaggering bravado as little more than "walking and talking with an attitude."

Even though Alan and Patty had planned this trip as good, close family time, David's every word and action declared that it was definitely "not cool" to be on vacation with his parents.

Yet, not long after the family had left the big city, not long after they had left behind the television, telephone, and computer games, not long after they had settled in at the cabin by the lake in the north woods, an amazing transformation took place.

David became calm and peaceful. He stopped struggling with his own pretentiousness and flamboyance. He stopped boasting and "knowing it all." He stopped preening and posturing. He was, once again, in the eyes of his parents, his fun-loving, happy, true self.

This is not to portray parents who want to stifle or impede their son's growth and maturity. This is not to describe parents who want their "little boy" back at the cost of his natural development. For, Alan and Patty well understand, appreciate, and support their son's evolving needs.

This is to describe a young man who came back to himself when he came back to nature—to the place of his origin. This is to tell of a young man who, instead of being "grounded" by his parents for unacceptable behavior, became "grounded" *in himself* when he literally returned to the ground—to the source of his being. This is to affirm the inextricable connection—the deep and powerful sense of unity—between human beings and the earth, which gives us life, sustenance, and purpose.

For at least a short while in the always tumultuous teenage voyage toward adulthood, David's journey back to the source reconnected him to the one vibration of existence and brought him—what you and your children can have when *you* connect with the source—self-awareness, self-assurance, and inner peace.

Consider the Works of Human Creation

An old legend teaches that when all the works of creation were completed, God asked the angels what they thought of the handiwork.

"Only one thing is lacking," they said. "It is the sound of praise to the Creator."

Plant a Garden

When you and your children plant a garden, you bring renewed purpose and new beauty to your little corner of the world.

Digging deep into the soil, you can feel your intimate connection to the ground and to the earth, and to the ever-renewing process of creation.

You and your children can soon come to know your cosmic importance in the ongoing natural order. You can understand the injunction of the ancient sage who insisted that, "if you are planting, and you hear that the messiah has come, *first* finish planting, then go to greet the messiah."

When you and your children plant a garden, you can plant seeds that will last forever, continually renewing the work of creation.

So, the story continues, God created the whisper of the wind, the song of the birds, and the sounds of music, and planted a melody in the hearts of children.

By giving rise to the voice of melody, God added one more measure of beauty to the works of creation.

And it wasn't long before we human beings—always eager to imitate God—began to add our own new beauty to our world.

Soaring music, great art, unfolding drama, delicate dance, and sublime literature became the wonders of human creation.

The arts became the bridge of beauty between God and humankind.

The writer E. M. Forster explains the process. "In the creative state, a man is taken out of himself. He lets down, as it were, a bucket into his subconscious, and draws up something which is normally beyond his reach. He mixes this thing with his normal experiences and out of the mixtures he makes a work of art."

The great artist Pablo Picasso put it simply, "I do not seek. I find."

There is no objective standard for judging the merit or the worth of the arts. "Beauty is in the eye of the beholder."

The arts, in themselves, are amoral—neither good nor bad, right nor wrong.

But, the arts can add depth and beauty to the human experience.

As the world-renowned architect Frank Lloyd Wright observed, "Art is the soul of our civilization."

"Music," said Victor Hugo "expresses that which cannot be put into words and that which cannot remain silent."

"Of the making of books, there is no end," says the Bible, because literature is the repository of the human experience, just as theater has become the mirror reflecting the human condition.

And "dance," said Ted Shawn, "is the only art of which we ourselves are the stuff of which it is made."

You can teach your children to experience the splendor of human creation when they immerse themselves in the soul-filling beauty of the arts.

The beauty of the universe is within each and every human being. It is, as W. Somerset Maugham said, "an ecstasy. It is as simple as hunger."

When the beauty within bubbles to the surface and seeks expression, it adds to the marvels of the world and the wonders of existence.

You can show your children how to fashion anew when you encourage them to let their own imaginations run wild and their creativity flow freely.

Go to a Museum

When you take your children to a museum—or to a concert, a recital, or the theater—you expose them to the great discoveries and the great creations of humankind.

When you hand them a fine book, you introduce them to the great thoughts and ideas of human civilization.

When you open your children's eyes and ears to the arts, you reveal to them beauties and wonders of human making, sourced by the Divine.

When you give your children the gift of human handiwork, you show them how to renew their souls and fill their hearts.

You can give them the time and the tools—the scissors, crayons, and paints; the musical instruments and ballet shoes; the blank pieces of paper and sharpened pencils; the stage on which to perform—to create far beyond the limits of beeping video games and glitzy computer programs.

You can give them, in the words of the writer Sherwood Anderson—literally if you can, figuratively if you must—"an attic to explore the past, and a basement to tinker with the future."

You can teach your children the words of Kahlil Gibran, "We live only to discover beauty. All else is a form of waiting."

Giving Thanks

The glories of the universe surround us and are within us.

Yet—in our fast-paced, super-sophisticated world—it is all too easy to take them for granted.

We listen, but do we really hear? Our eyes are open, but do we really see? Our hearts beat out the rhythm of life, but are we aware? Our entire beings are infused with the radiant, infinite goodness of creation, but do we appreciate?

Words of real admiration and sincere appreciation are sometimes hard to express. Words of praise and thanksgiving are sometimes difficult to utter.

You can teach your children to look beyond themselves; to acknowledge the spirit greater than themselves; to humbly and joyfully express gratitude and give thanks for all their many blessings.

In the words of the modern poet Ruth Brin, you can teach your children to give thanks "for the blessings You bestow openly, and for those You give in secret. . . . For the blessings I recognize, and for those I fail to recognize. . . . For the blessings that surround me on every side."

You can teach your children that their gratitude will delight their Creator, but that their words are just as much for them. For in their prayer is their greatness and their humility.

It takes a great person to be able to say, "Thank you; I appreciate you." It takes a humble person to know that s/he must.

Children of the Universe

Over the course of many months, an elderly bed-ridden father sent his children to the orchards to check on his favorite fruit trees.

"Describe the tree to me," he instructed each child.

The oldest son said, "I am sorry to tell you this, Father, but the tree looks like a burnt, barren stump."

His brother disagreed completely. "The tree," he said, "is full of lush green foliage."

The daughter said, "You are both wrong. The tree's branches are full of colorful blossoms."

And the youngest daughter said, "All three of you are wrong. The tree is bending under the weight of sweet fruit."

The father looked at his four children and said, "You are all right. For each of you saw the tree in a different season."

Your children can be children of all the earth's seasons, when they embrace the glorious universe in which they live, appreciate its wonders, and continually give thanks.

Your children can be children of all the earth's seasons, when they affirm the teaching of Sun Bear of the Chippewa Tribe who said, "I do not think that the measure of a civilization is how tall its buildings of concrete are, but how well its people have learned to relate to their environment and to each other."

Your children can be children of all the earth's seasons—of all the earth's greatness—when they understand with Novalis that "the seat of the soul is where the inner world and the outer world meet."

A Story to Tell Your Children

Seeking Good Fortune

There was once a man whose life seemed filled with misfortune. Although he worked hard, he never had enough to eat, and, in the winter, his threadbare clothes and flimsy hut were not enough to keep him from being very cold. And he was lonely, for he had few friends and no wife or children.

One day the man said to himself, "Life is not fair to me. I am going off in search of God, to ask God to grant me good fortune." And so, he began his journey.

On his way, he came across a beautiful maiden. She asked, "Where are you going?"

He replied, "I am searching for God, to ask for good fortune."

The beautiful maiden said, "Oh, what a wonderful idea! You see, I have this lovely home and this beautiful garden. I have all the food I want to eat and fine clothes to wear. But, I have no husband to be my companion. Please ask God for good fortune for me too."

The man promised to do as the maiden asked, and he continued on his way. It was not long before he came to one of the strangest looking trees he had ever seen. Even though it was planted right at the riverside, it was all dried up. The tree saw the man coming and asked, "Where are you going?"

The man replied, "I am searching for God, to ask for good fortune."

The tree said, "Oh, what a good idea! You see, I am planted right here by this gently flowing river, but my leaves never turn green—even in the springtime. Please ask God for good fortune for me too."

"I certainly will," said the man, and he continued on his journey. Before long, he came across a wolf sitting by the side of the road. The wolf asked, "Where are you going?"

The man said, "I am searching for God, to ask for good fortune."

"What a marvelous idea," said the wolf. "You see, I got lost from my pack, and now I am a lone wolf. I have no friends to play with or to hunt with. Please ask God for good fortune for me too."

The man agreed to talk to God about the wolf and went on his way.

The search for God took many more days, but, finally, the man found the place where God dwells.

He said, "God, my life has not been easy, so I have come to ask for good fortune for myself and for some friends I met along the way."

God listened, and said, "My child, I am giving you the gift of Good Fortune. Go, use it wisely and well." And God also gave the man gifts for the maiden, the tree, and the wolf.

With happiness in his heart, the man began his journey home. First, he came upon the wolf, and said, "God has given me a gift for you. God says that one day soon, someone will come to talk to you right here by the side of the road. This will be your new friend, who will play with you and hunt with you."

The wolf said, "You! My new friend must be you. Stay here and be my friend."

But the man said, "I would like to, but I have been given the gift of Good Fortune. I must go seek my fortune." And he left the wolf by the side of the road.

Next, the man came upon the tree, and said, "God has given me a gift for you. I am to tell you that the reason you are getting no water is that beneath your roots is buried a treasure chest filled with gold. As soon as the treasure is dug up, water will begin to flow, and your leaves will be green again."

"How wonderful!" said the tree. "Please dig up the treasure chest for me, and I will share all the gold with you."

But the man said, "I would like to, but I have been given the gift of Good Fortune. I must go seek my fortune." And he left the tree by the side of the river.

Almost home, the man came to the maiden's house, and said, "God has given me a gift for you. God wants you to know that one day very soon you will meet a man who will be your husband, and you will be very happy together."

The maiden said, "It must be you. You are the man that God has sent. Stay here and be my husband, and share my house and my garden with me."

But the man said, "I would like to, but I have been given the gift of Good Fortune. I must go and seek my fortune." And the man left and made his way home.

A year passed, and the man had not yet found good fortune. He decided to return to God to learn why the gift of Good Fortune had not come to him.

On his way, he met the maiden, who was still not married. She decided to go with him to ask God why her husband had not come. Together, they came to the tree, whose leaves were still brown and dry. The tree said, "Take one of my branches with you on your journey to God, and ask why no one has come to dig up the treasure chest."

Finally, they came to the wolf, who was still alone and lonely. The wolf decided to go on the journey to God, to find out why a friend had not yet appeared.

When they came to God, the man said, "We do not understand. You gave me the gift of Good Fortune, but good fortune has not come. You told the wolf that he would find a friend, but the friend has not appeared. You told the tree that water would flow when the treasure chest was dug up, but no one has come to dig. You told the maiden that soon she would be married, but no man has come to be her husband. Why, God? Why?"

And God laughed that sad, little laugh that only God can laugh, and said, "My children, My children. Open your eyes, and look. See what you have been given. See what you already have. See what good fortune is right before you."

And the man, the maiden, the tree branch, and the wolf finally understood, and, quietly, but joyfully, each said:

"Thank you, God."

"Thank you, God."

"Thank you, God."

"Thank you, God."

Questions to Discuss with
Your Children About Gratitude

A Question to Discuss with Your Children (Ages 4–8)

Your friend tells you that his family never celebrates Thanksgiving and wonders why your family celebrates this holiday.

What do you say?

A Question to Discuss with Your Youngsters (Ages 9–12)

You are on school field trip, and you just found out that a few of the kids have brought along their pocket knives and are planning to carve their names in a tree.

Do you tell a teacher? Why? Why not? What do you say to your classmates?

A Question to Discuss with Your Teenagers

Your principal refuses to institute a recycling program at your school. She says that it will take up too much of the staff's time, and take up too much storage space. She also says that the program will not provide enough money to the school to make all the effort worthwhile. You think recycling is a good idea. You are given five minutes to make your case to the principal that the school should start the recycling program.

What do you say? If she still refuses, what do you do?

A Prayer for the Earth

We call upon the earth, our planet home;
We call upon the mountains, the summits of silence;
We call upon the waters that rim the earth;
and we ask:
Teach us and show us the way.

We call upon the land which grows our food;
We call upon the forests that reach to the skies;
We call upon the creatures of the fields who share our home;
and we ask:
Teach us and show us the way.

We call upon all who have lived on this earth;
We call upon all that we hold most dear;
We call upon the Great Spirit that flows through all the universe;
and we ask:
Teach us and show us the way.

Chinook Blessing Litany adapted by W. D.

*"Get a Teacher;
Acquire a Friend"*

The Ethic of
FRIENDSHIP

A Zen student, hoping to become a teacher, studied with the master for ten years. After this time of apprenticeship, he felt ready to teach.

The young student came to the master for his blessing. It was a rainy day, so when he entered the master's house, the student left his umbrella and his wooden clogs outside.

The student said, "Master, I am ready to teach, and I have come for your blessing."

The master asked, "You left your umbrella and your clogs outside, didn't you?"

"Yes," replied the student.

"Did you place your umbrella to the left or to the right of your clogs?"

The student stood confused and flushed, for he could not remember.

And the master said, "The time of learning has not yet ended."

To Learn

It used to be that formal education in this country—especially a university degree—meant that a student was exposed to the entire gamut of human inquiry and discourse.

Now, diplomas and degrees signify the mastery of a particular curriculum, a specific field of study, a single subject.

Most high schools still evaluate the expression of educational excellence by the mastery of algebra and geometry.

And except for a few unique colleges and universities that still teach a "core curriculum," most students who leave the finest institutions of higher learning have expertise in one subject, but remain culturally illiterate—never having been taught the broad, full sweep of history, literature, philosophy, and the arts.

And even the finest formal education leaves much still to be learned.

The old saying puts it succinctly: "A college education never hurt anyone who was willing to learn something afterward."

Once, the genius inventor of the radio, Marconi, stayed up all night with a friend discussing the intricate aspects of wireless communication.

As dawn was breaking, Marconi said, "All my life I have been studying this matter, but there is one thing I simply cannot understand about radio."

"Something *you* do not understand about radio?" said his astonished friend. "Impossible! What is it?"

Said Marconi, "Why does it work?"

You can teach your children that learning never ends, for there is no end to learning.

Learning What Really Counts

Yet even the best schooling—what used to be called "book learning"—is severely limited. **"Education," it is said, "requires a lot of books. Wisdom requires a lot of time."**

A Plea to Parents

Work within your community to insist—to demand—that your schools give your children the very best education. They need it. They deserve it.

And, if your schools fail, then *you* must ensure educational excellence for your children. Teach them yourself; get them tutors; ask your church, synagogue, mosque, or youth center to provide supplemental educational programs.

Do whatever you can. Do whatever you must.

We cannot afford to have another generation that ranks last among children of the western world in educational achievement. We cannot afford to lose one more child—certainly not your child—to illiteracy, ignorance, or mediocrity.

Your children are counting on you.

A young man came to a master and asked, "How long is it going to take me to attain enlightenment?"

The master replied, "Ten years."

The young man was astonished. "So long?"

The master said, "I am sorry. I have made a mistake. It will take you twenty years."

The young man asked, "Why did you double the number of years it will take me to attain enlightenment?"

Said the master, "Now that I think about it, in your case, it will probably be thirty years."

Where does a person acquire not learning, but wisdom?

Take a Course

When you take a course, you show your children your love of learning, and that learning never stops.

You can take a course either toward a diploma or a degree that you never got, or toward an advanced degree, or as a way of acquiring new skills and expanding your knowledge. But, whatever your goal, you show your children your commitment to growth through education with the time and the hard work that it takes to successfully complete your study.

Can you think of any better way to impress upon your children the lifelong importance of learning than when they can ask you, "Have you done your homework yet?"

How does a person learn to use and sharpen the ability to think, to understand, to discern?

What teacher will touch not only a person's mind, but heart?

Where does a person learn to translate dreams into reality?

How does a person break away from self-imposed boundaries and tap into the limitless potential of mind and body?

When they are young, your children see you not only as sustainer and nurturer, but as sage and hero.

You are "bigger than life."

You know the answers to all their questions. You can explain the mysteries of their little world. You keep them safe from the dangers that threaten them. You protect them from the monsters who come out in the night.

If you are wise and skillful—and extremely fortunate—in those early years you can try to establish the rapport and trust that will transcend your role as "Mommy" or "Daddy," so that, as they grow, your children will still want your advice and counsel.

But, by the time they are teenagers, most children think that they "know it all" and are sure that their parents "know nothing." Most are like Mark Twain who, when he was seventeen, thought his father to be the stupidest man in the world. When he was twenty-one, he was amazed at how much the old man had learned in four short years.

You would like your children to continually turn to you for guidance and direction because you have so much to give them, so much to teach, so much to impart.

Especially in the years when they are trying and testing their growing freedom and independence, especially in the years when they think that they are so autonomous and strong—and you know that they are so vulnerable and tender—you want them to benefit from your lifetime of knowledge and experience.

You can always show your children that you still have much to teach and that they still have much to learn.

One night, a father decided that his daughter was now old enough to go to the barn and feed the horses.

But the girl was afraid.

So her father took his daughter out to the front porch of the house and lit a lantern, held it up, and asked her how far she could see by the lantern's light.

"I can see halfway down the path," she said.

"Fine," said her father. "Now carry this lantern halfway down the path."

The young girl did as she was told, and when she reached her destination, her father asked her, "Now how far can you see by the lantern's light?"

His daughter called back that she could now see to the gate.

"Good," said her father. "Now walk to the gate."

Once again, the girl did as she was told, and when she reached the gate, her father asked, "Now how far can you see?"

"I can see the barn," came the girl's reply.

"Wonderful," called out the father. "Now walk to the barn and open the door."

The girl did just as her father told her, and, finally, she shouted back that she was at the barn and could see the horses.

"Excellent," her father called. "Now feed the horses."

And he stepped back into the house.

Teaching Through Being

You may still be afraid that, unlike the hero-struck tykes your children once were, and unlike the somewhat malleable youngsters they can sometimes be, most children reach a stage when they will simply not listen to you anymore.

So, what is a parent to do?

You can still give your wisdom to your children—you can still influence their thinking and their behavior—if you do not fall into the "parent trap" of thinking that *you* "know it all."

When your children accuse you of "not knowing anything," rather than trying to convince them that you do, show them that they are right. Show them that you *don't* know everything.

No parental "job description" demands perfection. You do not have to be the archetypal "knight in shining armor" or "wise queen" forever.

You can let your children see your failings and your foibles. You can let them touch your hurts and your vulnerabilities. You can let them know about your shattered dreams and about the fears that keep you awake at night.

You can show your children that you are—as they will always be—a "work in progress"—a human being who tries and tries again, sometimes tasting the sweetness of success, sometimes choking on the bitterness of failure.

You can show your children that you want to constantly grow and develop; that you want to enhance your strengths and perfect your imperfections.

You can show your children that you are always eager to learn; that you do not rely merely on your own good counsel, but that you seek wisdom and enlightenment from teachers and guides, masters and mentors. As the Buddha taught, "When the student is ready, the Master appears."

You can show your children that the compelling questions of life, the matters of mind and heart, the hopes and the dreams, the journeys to new frontiers, are never completely answered but are all part of a continuing dialogue of exploration and anticipation.

When I left my full-time job as a congregational rabbi to become a full-time teacher, writer, and lecturer, my children were shaken and concerned.

All their lives, I had worked in a particular setting and fulfilled a specific role. Now, that familiarity, that structure, that stability, was being upset. My children wanted to know: If I weren't the rabbi, what would my identity be? If I didn't go to the synagogue every day, where would my place be? If I didn't officiate at services and weddings and funerals, what would my function be? If I didn't have a job, what would my income be?

I could have simply said, "Don't worry, boys. Everything is going to be just fine. Trust me."

But, that would have been a "macho" lie. And my sons—intuitive and wise—would have seen through my ruse.

Instead, I shared with them my desire and my need for this mid-career change. I told them about both the joys and the frustrations of a two-decade life of service to God and to community—although having lived with me and the job for all those years, they understood as much and more than I could tell them.

I told them of the new ways I wanted to work and serve, the new avenues for sharing my ideas and visions, the new outlets for my imagination and creativity, the new dreams that could now be spoken, and the new hopes that could be fulfilled.

And I told them all about my hesitations and my concerns and my fears.

I introduced them to the new teachers and guides in my life, the people whose wisdom and experience would help me shape and forge a new path.

And although they—and I—were still worried—for change is difficult and scary—they understood and respected what I was doing. And they encouraged me through the early moments—supporting me in my painful failures and cheering me in my first tentative successes.

Rather than "shutting out" my children from one of the most important decisions of my life, I shared with them the truth and the process. They knew of the risks and of the potential rewards. I trusted them with my feelings, and they, in turn, trusted me in my choices.

And, hopefully, they learned a bit about being honest with themselves and open with others, about taking risks and having courage, about being bold and trusting their instincts, and, most of all, about chasing their own dreams.

You can show your children that when they—like you—are always open to growth, when they follow their hearts, when they find the ones who will guide them, when they drink in enlightened words of teaching and counsel, they—like you—will walk toward wisdom.

The devotee knelt to be initiated into discipleship.

The guru whispered the sacred mantra into his ear, with the stern warning that it was not to be revealed to anyone.

"What if I reveal the mantra?" asked the devotee.

The guru replied, "Anyone to whom you reveal the sacred mantra will be relieved from ignorance and suffering. But *you* will be excluded from discipleship, and you will suffer damnation."

As soon as he heard the guru's words, the devotee rushed into the marketplace, collected a large crowd around him, and shouted the sacred mantra for everyone to hear.

The other disciples immediately reported his action to the guru and demanded that the new devotee be expelled from the monastery.

Be a Mentor

Whatever your situation, whatever your status in life, there is someone out there who needs your wisdom, your experience, your guidance.

Perhaps it is a younger sibling; perhaps a neighbor or a friend; perhaps a colleague at work; perhaps a co-worker in a community organization; perhaps someone at your church, synagogue, or mosque; or perhaps someone in a self-help group.

When you share your counsel, when you share yourself with someone who needs you—when you become a mentor—you immeasurably enrich the life of the person who has come to you for help. And you give back to the never-ending circle of learning and teaching, for you understand the wisdom of the rabbinic sage who said, "I have learned much from my teachers, but I have learned even more from my students."

The guru smiled and said, "This man has no need of anything I can teach him. His action has shown him to be a guru in his own right."

When you show your children that you are real—instead of the heroic childhood image they may still carry, but which is bound to disappoint—you become a much more credible, much more reliable voice. For no matter what the hardship or how great the disillusionment along the way, fellow "strugglers" respect and learn from each other's journey—and often—if not in body, then surely, in spirit—continue forward on the journey together.

Connecting

The very same sentence of ancient wisdom that advises, "get a teacher," continues by saying, "and acquire a friend."

The sages understood that teachers and mentors train the intellect, touch the heart, and inspire the spirit. But beyond that most profound of bonds is one of the most precious of all human gifts—the deep soul connection of intimate and faithful friendship.

The poet said, "I looked for my soul / But my soul I could not see. / I looked for my God / But my God eluded me. / I looked for a friend / And then I found all three."

Kahlil Gibran put it most simply, "Your friend is your needs answered."

He probably knew friends like these.

"My friend is not back from the battlefield, sir," one soldier said. "Request permission to go out and get him."

"Permission denied," said the officer. "I don't want you to risk your life for a man who is probably dead."

Disobeying orders, the soldier went anyway. An hour later, he returned, carrying the corpse of his friend, but mortally wounded himself.

The officer was filled with grief. "I told you he was dead," he said. "Now I've lost both of you. Tell me, was it worth going out there to bring in a corpse?"

"Oh, it was sir," the dying man replied. "You see, when I got to him, he was still alive, and he said to me, 'Jack, I was sure that you would come.'"

You can teach your children that the human quest is to find the relationships, to form the friendships, that will give them connection and intimacy, responsibility and commitment, satisfaction and deep, deep joy.

Extending

Life-cycle events and, especially, holidays used to be celebrated in the midst of large, extended families.

In the movie *Avalon,* which portrays youngsters growing up in just such a large, close-knit family in post-war Baltimore, the family tradition is to gather for holiday meals.

"Make New Friends, but Keep the Old"

It used to be that making and keeping friends was easy. Your friends were the people in your neighborhood—the same people you went to school with, played with, and worked with. The kids who were your classmates in kindergarten often became the friends of a lifetime.

Now, in this incredibly fast-paced, mobile world, it is much harder to find and make a cherished friend because making and keeping friends takes time and emotional energy—which few have and even fewer are willing to invest.

When you show your children that you make the effort to nurture and keep old friendships, when you show your children that you are ready to spend the time and the energy that it takes to make and sustain new friendships, you show them the value of friends and the benefit of mutual commitment.

When you show your children what it takes to have a friend, you show them what it is to be a friend.

One uncle is always late for the celebration and, year after year, the family waits for him to appear before beginning the festive feast.

One year, the family decides that it will no longer cater to the tardy relative. When he does not show up on time, they begin without him.

Uncle walks into the house, sees the meal already in progress, and cries out—in real indignation and pain—"You cut the turkey without me! You cut the turkey without me!"

It takes decades before the uncle's pride is soothed, so the family rift can heal.

Great family traditions—and the legendary, almost holy, memories that come with them—are slowly dying because parents, grandparents, children, and grandchildren no longer live in the "old neighborhood."

The closest of blood relatives are often flung across the country and the world, unable to be with each other on holidays and sacred occasions, connected only by a telephone call and a tug at the heart of their collective longings.

That is why deep friendships take on a new and vital role in the human community.

Now, special moments are very often observed not with the extended family of birth, but with the "extended family" of friends.

Rather than dozens of aunts, uncles, cousins, and second cousins filling the "family homestead" for Thanksgiving or a birthday party, friends join together—at your house this year and my house next year—to observe and celebrate.

You can teach your children that friends can be with each other at life's most important and significant moments: sharing in commemoration; celebrating in joy; comforting in sorrow; creating shared memories and mutual histories.

In Friendship

You can teach your children that in friendship is selfless devotion—given and received.

An observer saw a woman in a hospital gently cleaning the sores on the festering body of her friend.

"I wouldn't do that for a million dollars," he said.

Without pausing in her work, the woman replied, "Neither would I."

As Paramahansa Yogananda has put it, "There is a magnet in your heart which will attract true friends. That magnet is unselfishness, thinking of others first. . . . When you learn to live for others, they will live for you."

Create New Traditions

Childhood memories rooted in family traditions often bring warmth and comfort—and meaningful direction—to adulthood.

If your family cannot gather together often to share in life events and holiday celebrations, then you can join with your friends to commemorate special occasions and significant moments. And you can show your children that life's grandest moments can be that much more beautiful and meaningful when shared by loving friends.

And together, you and your friends—your children and theirs—can create new rituals and new traditions that give definition and meaning to your shared observances.

You and your friends can teach your children the wisdom of the poet who taught, "Light tomorrow with today."

For as your children join you in creating personal rituals and new traditions of celebration, they can seed and nourish the very memories that will delight and sustain them when they are grown up—and when they begin the process all over again with their children.

Or, as E. W. Howe put it, "When a friend is in trouble, don't annoy him by asking if there is anything you can do. Think up something appropriate and do it."

You can teach your children that in friendship is the place where secrets can be told and heard, where confidences can be spoken and absorbed, where fears can be admitted and shared.

And you can teach your children that in friendship is the mirror of truth, which will always be held before their eyes so that they can see themselves clearly.

The stark truth of these words—a truth that both frightens and consoles—became, once again, vividly apparent to me when I gave friends and colleagues copies of the manuscript of this book to read and critique.

Who are my friends, the people I look to for guidance and direction, for candor wrapped in gentleness and honesty tempered with kindness? Who are the people I trust to put my interests and needs above their own, to be loving critics, to be emotionally available, supportive and encouraging?

Who are the people for whom I would do exactly the same, without a moment's hesitation, on a moment's notice?

One is a friend I have known since we were seven years old; another, since we were fifteen. One is a colleague with whom I went to undergraduate and rabbinical school more than twenty-five years ago. Two are professional colleagues with whom I have worked during the past twenty years. One is a Catholic priest, a teaching colleague at the university. Two are new friends, whom I have met in very recent years. One is my life partner, my wife.

With each, I have a special and unique relationship, based on our shared experiences and our mutual respect. With all, I share deep love and abiding commitment.

Over the years, we have shared much of what life has to offer: we have danced at weddings and comforted at divorce; we have rejoiced at the birth of children and watched them grow; we have buried parents; we have laughed and celebrated personal and professional triumphs; and we have wept and caught each other's tears at moments of bitter defeat.

These are my friends—the people to whom I open my heart, the people with whom I risk, the people to whom I entrust all that is most precious to me.

I gave them my manuscript to read—as I give them my life to share—knowing that in their souls I will see a reflection of my soul.

For my children—and yours—I hope and pray for friends like these—friends Kahlil Gibran described as the people "you come to with your hunger and seek (them) for peace."

You can teach your children that in friendship, there is the whole of the human condition—triumph, laughter, and love; the possibility of great joy and happiness, but also tragedy, bitterness, and sorrow; the potential for deep hurt and pain.

Being a friend can be one of life's most fulfilling—and most difficult—tasks.

As with all human relationships, even the best friendship will have its sublime moments of transcendence and radiance, and its wretched moments of disillusionment, anger, and despair.

Yet, a great friendship is worth all the work it takes to preserve and endure, for real friends understand the wisdom of the Native American proverb that teaches, "The soul would have no rainbow, if the eyes had no tears."

You can teach your children that in friendship is loyalty—the faithful commitment of one human being to another.

Blind loyalty is dangerous. Unchecked, it can lead to fundamentalism and anarchy, and, in this generation, to Nazis burning up little babies in crematoria.

Yet, well modulated, loyalty can be one of the sweetest of life's virtues—signaling trust, faith, fidelity, and devotion.

Josiah Royce warned, "Unless you can find some sort of loyalty, you cannot find unity and peace."

Or to put it quite succinctly, "Whoever eats my bread, sings my song."

"Root, Root, Root for the Home Team"

If you grew up rooting for the Chicago Cubs or the Boston Red Sox, you know what it means to remain loyal to the home team—no matter how often they lose or how seldom they win.

When you show your children your loyalties—not just to your home team, but to your friends—you teach them personal allegiance and devotion.

When you show your children that you maintain your loyalties regardless of situation or circumstance, ignoring outside opinion, not succumbing to coercion or pressure, you teach them abiding dedication and commitment.

When you show your children what it means to be resolute, firm, and unswerving in your friendships, you show them your honor and teach them to affirm theirs.

So They Will Be Known

You can teach your children that when a person stands for good, he is sometimes opposed by people who stand for evil; when a person demands decency and integrity, she is sometimes opposed by people who advocate wickedness and corruption.

That is why the old proverb teaches that "A man is not only known by the company he keeps, but by the enemies he makes."

You can teach your children that when their principles are at stake, or their sense of moral right is violated, they can proudly count their enemies and wear that enmity as a badge of honor.

Yet, you can also teach your children that an enemy need not be an enemy forever.

You can teach them that if they prevail, they can act graciously. As the Dutch proverb teaches, "When your enemy retreats, make him a golden bridge."

Even better, you can teach them the wisdom of Abraham Lincoln who wisely asked, "Am I not destroying my enemies when I make friends of them?"

The Face of Friendship

The master asked his disciples how they could tell when the night had ended and the day had begun.

One said, "When you see an animal in the distance and can tell if it is a horse or a cow."

"No," said the master.

Another said, "When you look at a tree in the distance and can tell if it is a fig tree or a peach tree."

"Wrong again," said the master.

"Well, then," the students demanded, "when is it?"

And the master replied, "When you look at the face of man or woman, and see that he is your brother, she is your sister. For, if you cannot do this, then no matter what time it is by the sun, it is still night."

The faces of your brothers and sisters, your heart friends, are before you and your children—mirroring your own faces right back at you.

In every friend, in every friendship, you can see and reflect the beauty of human connection and the value of human commitment, the intimacy of human love, and the passions of every human soul.

In every friend, in every friendship, you can see and reflect a life as precious as your own.

And in every friend, in every friendship, you can see and reflect a vision of hope for the whole world: the time when billions of individual people will seek each other in kinship and friendship, and weave a multi-hued fabric of respect, good will, and affection.

A Story to Tell Your Children

Two Friends

Once upon a time, there were two very good friends—Samuel and Jacob. They lived near one another, they studied together, they spent most of their time with each other.

After they had grown up, gotten married, and had children of their own, Samuel moved away to another country. Still, they wanted to continue their friendship. So they made a pledge that they would try to visit each other once each year.

Once in his travels, Jacob came near to the city where Samuel lived. Naturally, he wanted to see his long-time friend.

But Jacob did not know if a visit would be possible, for Samuel's country was at war with another country. And it was very dangerous to be anywhere near Samuel's city at that time.

Jacob came to Samuel's city at nightfall, but before he could find his old friend's house, he was arrested by the secret police, who charged him with being a spy who had come to steal military secrets.

Jacob was brought to trial immediately, found guilty, and sentenced to be hanged from the gallows. What a terrible fate for someone who had just wanted to visit his old friend!

Jacob was very sad as he sat in his jail cell, awaiting his hanging. He thought of his wife and his little children, and he wept bitter tears.

When the time came for Jacob's hanging, as was the custom in that country, the king came to watch. Seeing the king, Jacob fell to his knees, and cried out, "Your Majesty, gracious King, I am innocent of any wrongdoing. I did not commit these horrible crimes, and yet, I have been given this cruel punishment. Please, merciful King, I ask one favor of you. Please give me one week to return to my home, to set my affairs in order, to bid farewell to my wife and my children, and to provide for my family's future. I give you my word, my solemn pledge and promise, that I will return in one week and face my fate."

The king laughed. He said, "My courts have said that you are a spy. Now you ask me to grant you a one-week leave? How do I know that your promise is worth anything? How can I be sure that you will return?"

Before Jacob could answer the king, a man pushed his way through the crowd.

"Good King," he said, "I will be this man's pledge. I will take his place in jail, and if he does not return in one week, as he has promised, you may hang me instead."

The king was astonished. He said, "Who are you, and why do you offer yourself in place of this prisoner?"

The man replied, "My name is Samuel. This man, Jacob, has been my friend since we were children. I know that he is a good man. And I know that trouble has befallen him in our city only because he came to visit me and honor our friendship. I trust him. If he says he will return, then he will return. So, let him go take care of his household, and I will remain in his place."

The king was so moved by Samuel's words that he agreed. Jacob was freed to go home for a week, and Samuel was put in jail.

The week passed. The gallows were ready. The time for the hanging came. But, Jacob did not return.

The sun began to set, and darkness began to fall. Still, Jacob had not returned—not that anyone in the city expected him to. The king and the noblemen came to the town square, and a large crowd gathered to see the outcome of this strange case.

Samuel was brought from the jail and stood at the gallows. Night fell; the moon appeared; stars twinkled in the sky. The king gave the order, "Let the hanging take place." The hangman put the noose around Samuel's neck.

Suddenly, a loud cry was heard, "Wait, wait. I am here. Do not harm my friend. I am here to receive my own punishment."

And there was Jacob, making his way through the crowd. He was rushing to his own hanging, in order to save his friend.

The people in the crowd cheered and clapped their hands.

The king was so touched by the great loyalty of the two friends that he said, "Because of your true friendship, I will pardon the stranger. He may go free."

Then, turning to Jacob and Samuel, the king added, "There is only one thing I ask. Let me be the third friend of the two of you."

Questions to Discuss with Your Children About Friendship

A Question to Discuss with Your Children (Ages 4–8)

Your best friend just told you that he hates you and never wants to talk to you or see you again.

How do you feel? What do you do?

A Question to Discuss with Your Youngsters (Ages 9–12)

You are a talented young musician—or artist, or dancer, or computer whiz. You take special classes from a master teacher, who accepts only the finest students. Your friend wants to get into your class and asks you to recommend her to the teacher. You don't think that your friend has the talent or the ability to be in the class, but you know that your opinion will carry a lot of weight with your teacher.

What do you do?

A Question to Discuss with Your Teenagers

Your good friend has been very depressed lately. On the phone last night, she told you that she is thinking about killing herself. She said that she has enough pills to "do the job." Then she said, "If you are really my friend, you won't say a word about this to anyone."

What do you do?

A Prayer for
Teachers and Friends

To the teachers and the guides,
and to the students and their students,
to all who teach and learn,
in this place and every place,
to them and to us,
Life!

To friends and companions,
brothers and sisters of soul and heart,
to all who give and receive,
who share and who trust,
in this place and every place,
to them and to us,
Love!

We ask You, O God,
for grace, loving kindness and mercy,
for them and for us,
now and forever.

Amen and Amen.

Inspired by *Kaddish D'Rabbanan,*
the Jewish Prayer for Scholars;
adapted by W. D.

The *The* **8**TH

GOLDEN RULE

"Dwell Together in Unity"

The Ethic of
PEACE

For many years, two men lived on neighboring farms. They were the best of friends, and they often helped each other with the planting and the harvesting.

One day, one said to the other, "You know, in all the years we have known each other, we have never quarreled. We have never even spoken a harsh word to each other. For once, why don't we try to argue, just like other people do?"

His friend replied, "I don't even know how a quarrel happens. What do we do?"

The first man thought for a few minutes, and then he said, "I know. We don't have any fences between our properties. Let's argue about that parcel of land over there. Even though I know it belongs to you, I'll say that it is mine. Then we can have a fight, just like other people."

So the man did just that. He said, "You see that parcel of land. It is mine."

The neighbor replied, "No, it is mine."

The first man countered, "No, I am sure it is mine."

And his friend replied, "All right. If you are so sure it is yours, I believe you. It is yours." And he walked away, unable to fight.

The Source of Strife

Countries do not do battle.

Nations do not declare war.

Political ideology is not sacred scripture, and national boundaries were not carved into the land at the moment of creation.

Human beings—individual men and women, born with good hearts—somehow learn enough bigotry and hatred, enough antipathy and enmity, to grow up to become the kings and presidents and generals who send themselves—and their sons and daughters—off to combat, to kill and be killed.

You can teach your children that there can be peace when there are no soldiers who will fight, no generals who will command, no presidents who will declare war.

For as the medieval philosopher Baruch Spinoza taught, "Peace is not an absence of war, it is a virtue, a state of mind. . . ."

You can teach your children that there is peace in the world when there is peace within nations. There is peace within nations when there is peace in communities. There is peace in communities when there is peace within homes. And there is peace within homes when there is peace in individual hearts.

Peace Through Understanding

You can teach your children that a good, decent, ethical person works for peace by understanding and empathizing with others.

The story is told of the people who were warned of a great earthquake that would swallow up all the waters of the land. Drinking the new waters that would take their place—the people were admonished—would make everyone silly and foolish.

But what could they do? They must drink water in order to live. So, whatever might happen, the people decided that they would drink the new waters.

Only the king was worried about the consequences. So before the earthquake, he carried huge jugs of safe water up to his mountain retreat, so that he would have enough pure water to last him until the day he died.

Soon the earthquake came, and the waters vanished. The new water filled every ocean, lake, river, stream, and pond.

A few months later, the king came down the mountain to see what had happened.

Everyone had, indeed, become foolish.

But they attacked him, for *he* was the one who was different. All the people thought that the king was the one who was silly.

So the king went back up the mountain, happy for the water he had saved.

But as time went by, he found his loneliness unbearable. He yearned for human company, and so he went down the mountain again.

Once again, he was rejected by the people, for he was so different from them.

The king went back up the mountain, and it took only one more day for him to decide. He threw away all the water he had saved, drank the new water, and joined all the people in their foolishness.

He was, again, in harmony with the human community.

Peace Through Acceptance

You can teach your children that a good, decent, ethical person brings peace by accepting the shortcomings and faults of others.

A woman decided to start a flower garden.

She prepared the soil and planted the seeds of many beautiful flowers.

But, when the garden bloomed, it was filled not just with the colorful flowers, but it was also overrun with dandelions.

The woman sought the advice of gardeners and tried every method to get rid of the dandelions, but nothing worked. The dandelions remained.

Have Family Meetings

When you have regular family meetings, you can show your children how to get in touch with their own feelings and needs, and how to listen to and respect the needs and feelings of others.

At your family meetings, you can teach your children to resolve conflict, to compromise, and to value peace over strife.

At your family meetings, everyone can have a voice and a vote. Yet, at the same time, in retaining your parental prerogative of veto power, you can teach your children the real-life lessons of how to accept defeat and deal with disappointment.

Your family meetings can be a microcosm of the world where your children can learn that it is better to find common ground than to do battle, better to negotiate than to fight. They can learn that the very best way to settle any potential conflict is to find the way for everyone to "win."

Finally, the woman went all the way to the neighboring town to speak to the area's most expert gardener.

The wise and experienced gardener had counseled many, and suggested a variety of remedies to the woman. But she had tried them all.

For a long while, the woman and the expert gardener sat in silence, each wondering how to solve the problem of the dandelions.

Finally, the gardener looked at the woman and said, "Well, I suggest you learn to love the dandelions."

You can tell your children that peace comes when they learn to love themselves and all the people whose lives they touch—the beautiful, colorful "flowers" they prize and cherish, and the "dandelions" they can come to love.

Peace Through Reconciliation

You can teach your children that a good, decent, ethical person brings peace by working to reconcile differences.

Many years ago, when my children were about six and eight years old, they came with me to the synagogue service one Saturday morning when their mother was at home not feeling well.

This was late in December, during the eight-day festival of Chanukah, and there were many people in the synagogue that day.

After the service and the *kiddush*—the "social hour" where my boys ate their fair share of cookies and brownies—I asked them to wait for me in my study while I greeted some more of the worshippers.

I later entered my study at the exact moment that Scott—the older boy—was hitting Seth over the head with a Chanukah candle—not the tiny candles that are used for home observances, but the large, heavy candles that are used on the pulpit.

I heard the "crack" of the candle on the head and the wail of pain coming from my younger son, and I jumped right into action. In one swoop, I cradled Seth's head, grabbed the candle from Scott's hand, and started yelling.

"What are you doing? You could kill your brother! What's wrong with you? Can't you come to synagogue one day without Mommy here and behave?

"That's it! You guys are really in trouble. Get your coats. We're going home. And you had better figure out a good way to explain this to Mommy!"

I quickly came up with the most compelling punishment I could think of.

"No Chanukah presents for you tonight."

The protests began immediately.

Seth: "What do you mean no Chanukah presents? I didn't do anything. He hit me. Why should I be punished?"

Scott: "You always take his side. You only saw the very last second of what went on. He's been bothering me and pinching me and hitting me since we got in here. Finally, I defended myself, and you are blaming me for the whole thing. It's not my fault. He started, not me."

Me: "Listen, you guys. This is totally inappropriate behavior. Brothers shouldn't fight like this, especially in synagogue. I'm sorry, but this is too serious to just forget. No Chanukah presents tonight."

Seth: "Not fair!"

Scott: "You always take his side because he's younger. You're not listening to me."

Me: "Let's go home."

Clearly, I didn't handle the situation too well.

I was scared that Seth could have been really hurt. And I was angry that my boys were behaving in such an outrageous way—especially in synagogue. After all, aren't the "PK," the "preacher's kids," supposed to be perfect little angels? What would the congregants say if they found out?

So we went home and told Mommy everything that had happened. She was just as upset as I was, and "upheld" the decision that there would be no Chanukah presents that night.

Lighting the candles that evening was a sad affair.

Yet, I thought that the starkness of the punishment—it was the first and only time in my children's lives that they did not receive a nightly Chanukah gift—would impress the severity of their behavior on them.

I was wrong.

For what I forgot to do was listen to my sons.

They had real issues that needed addressing. Seth felt unduly punished. Scott felt singled out because he claimed that Seth was more at fault than he was.

Both felt that the whole incident was just one more example of their continuing older brother–younger brother conflict and their parents' lack of response to their individuality and their separate needs.

Of course, I did not gather all these insights in the atmosphere of hostility and anger that permeated the house that afternoon. Nor did I learn any of this the next day or the next.

I was slowly "introduced" to this wisdom by my children.

As you can imagine, the "Chanukah candle, no Chanukah presents" incident became family lore, trotted out over the years as a reminder of my less than sterling job of parenting.

As Scott and Seth grew older and became more insightful and articulate, they were able to tell me what they had been feeling that day.

What I should have done was not just see the behavior, but listen for the causes that led to the behavior.

Then, I could have tried to reconcile their differences, to bring a harmony and peace to their relationship and ours.

But, I didn't. And a wonderful opportunity for good parenting—and an outstanding opportunity for peacemaking—was lost.

I invite you to not let similar opportunities pass you by.

This kind of listening, reconciliation, and peacemaking can happen anywhere, any time—in your workplace, with your spouse, with your friends, between you and your children.

Conflict and strife can give way to harmony and peace. And you can be the peacemaker.

Peace Through Letting Go

You can teach your children that a good, decent, ethical person works toward peace not by holding onto hurts or affronts, but by letting go and moving on.

Meditate & Mediate

Despite the unfair reputation given them in books and movies, and despite the horrible wars that they sometimes fought, the Native Americans who inhabited the plains and fields wanted to be peace-loving men and women.

So whenever possible, instead of letting conflict escalate to war, they would seek out their enemies, sit together, and attempt to work out their differences. They would seal their agreement by smoking a peace pipe.

When you meditate—or do yoga or martial arts or any other exercise that calms your mind—you show your children how to practice thinking gentle and peaceful thoughts.

And, then, you can show your children that you can mediate—that you can be the one working to overcome conflict and strife by bringing people together in harmony and tranquillity. From your gentle and peaceful thoughts can come gentle words and peaceful actions.

When you smoke the figurative peace pipe, you can show your children how to bring peace to their lives, and you can show them how to be the peacemaker.

Two monks journeying back to their monastery found an exceedingly beautiful woman standing helplessly at the edge of a fast-flowing river.

Without a word, the older monk picked her up, put her on his back, and carried her across. On the other side, he gently set her down. She smiled at him, bowed deeply, and continued on her way.

The monks, too, continued on their journey, but the younger monk could not contain himself. For the next two hours he berated his fellow.

"Have you forgotten our rules? How dare you touch a woman? How could you lift her and carry her across the river? Such behavior is entirely unsuitable for a monk. You have put us all into disrepute. What if someone had seen you? What would people say?"

The older monk listened patiently to the never-ending rebuke. As they neared the monastery, he finally broke his silence and said to his companion, "Brother, I left that woman back at the river bank. Are you still carrying her?"

A woman in a class I recently taught had a very practical application of the monk's question.

I asked the members of a class on Jewish ritual observances why they light candles on Friday evening to usher in the Sabbath.

One replied that she lights candles because the ritual laws of the Sabbath require it of her.

Another replied that the lighting of the candles marks the official welcoming of the Sabbath for her and her family.

A third said that she lights the candles out of a sense of tradition, following the custom that her mother and her grandmother before her had observed.

The fourth woman said that all the reasons given by the others were important to her, but she had one more to add. She said, "I can't begin the Sabbath, which is supposed to be a day of rest and peace, if I am feeling hurt or angry; if I am frustrated by things that went on at work; or if I am upset with my kids; or if I am mad at my husband. So, when I light the Sabbath candles each week, I have to let go of whatever anger I am feeling.

"Lighting the candles means that, at least once a week, I take a deep breath, let go of my anger, and start all over again. Only then, can I feel the peace of the Sabbath begin to envelop my home and my heart."

"Cast Your Bread upon the Waters"

There is a quaint Jewish custom passed on from the Middle Ages. On the afternoon of *Rosh HaShanah,* the Jewish new year, Jews gather near an ocean, river, or stream to symbolically "cast" their transgressions into the water to be carried away by the flowing currents. In this way, past mistakes are repented and "thrown away," and the new year is greeted with a fresh, "clean slate."

To symbolize the transgressions, bread crumbs or pebbles or pocket dust are cast into the water.

You can show your children how to let go of the hurts that still haunt them, the pains that still pursue them, the angers that still hold them, when you create your own little ceremony of "casting" away.

You can use bread crumbs thrown into a body of flowing water to show your children how to give up that which burdens their days and disturbs their nights.

You can show your children how to bring peace to their lives and serenity to their souls when you show them that holding on just hurts more, but that letting go sets their spirits free.

Peace comes, in the words of many contemporary spiritual teachers, when you "let go. And let God."

"I Cry 'Peace, Peace,' but There Is No Peace"

You can teach your children that a good, decent, ethical person works for peace because warfare brings too much human pain and suffering.

Whether it is on the playground, on the streets, or in far-off battlefields, modern technology puts the ravages of warfare right on the television set in your living room.

How often can you and your children see the carnage and the human anguish without being profoundly touched and moved to action?

Images come from all over the world—people dead and dying, little children starving to death, cities devastated, homes laid to waste.

Gunfire is heard across the globe; the nuclear saber is rattled constantly.

The dark, twisted faces of war haunt the planet.

And the continually recorded chronicle of humankind's inhumanity is your children's constant companion—shouted from newspaper headlines and served at dinner with the nightly news.

But, if Africa and Asia and Europe are too far away to seem real, to have any immediate impact on your children, they need look no further than their own backyards to experience hostility and anguish.

The week I was writing this chapter, a young man graduated from high school in San Diego. He had beaten the odds. Even though he was black, poor, and had been brought up by a single mother, he had risen above his background. He graduated at the top of his class with a straight "A" average and was president of his student government. He had been awarded a full four-year academic scholarship by a prestigious Ivy League university. He planned to go on to medical school.

On graduation night he was standing outside his home, quietly talking with a few friends, when a drive-by shooter opened fire. He was killed instantly. His promising future was snuffed out in a blood-splattered second.

Even as I write these words, this young man's mother's brokenhearted wail of agony—which was broadcast again and again on local television and radio stations—reverberates in my ears.

Demonstrate

You can demonstrate your commitment to peace when you show your government—local and national—and the governments of the world that you insist on living in a world of peace.

It is not as naive as it sounds.

Governments are of the *people,* by the *people,* and for the *people.* Every president and prime minister is someone's husband or wife, someone's mother or father. They are human beings with human feelings and emotions.

They understand, and they *will* listen.

Show your children that you will use every means at your disposal—demonstration, petition, protest, the power of the press and the power of the ballot box—to tell the people who make up the governments that you want a world of peace. Tell them, in the image of the 1960s, that if they make war, you will not come.

When you show your children how much a world of peace means to you, and how hard you are willing to work for it, you help create another generation committed to peace.

For, in your devotion to peace, your children will seek peace.

His story is unspeakably sad, yet, unfortunately, not unique. You could tell the same kind of story, over and over again, from the place where you live.

If this young man's snuffed-out life is at all representative of thousands of lives that are being lost across this country each year—and it is—then, perhaps, his story can be the incentive for you and your children to finally say, "Enough!"

Turn Off the Television—Again

The televised news reports of the real world are sad and disturbing enough.

Your young and impressionable children do not need to watch the hundreds of scenes of made-up television violence—murder, rape, and wars—that fill the screens every day.

Sociologists can argue forever whether watching violence on television leads to violent behavior. If it does, then surely it should not be watched. But, even if it does not, it endorses—if even passively—an attitude and an atmosphere that disregards the sanctity of human life and the preciousness of human relationships.

When you turn off the television, you show your children that they can thrive without violent images constantly dancing before their eyes, and that human violence should not be glorified or celebrated, or—worse—taken as ordinary and accepted as the norm.

When you turn off the television, you show your children that you—and they—can take the steps—small and personal though they be—to creating and living in a world of peace.

Enough warfare, enough violence, enough suffering, enough agony.

Peace does not come to those who simply hope and wait.

Peace comes when men and women of goodwill work for peace, by going to the places where peace is born. Peace comes when men and women of peace plant the seeds of peace; cultivate, nurture, and watch over peace; and create the environment where peace can grow and flourish.

Let There Be Peace

You can teach your children that real peace comes from within each and every human being, spreads outward to every other human being, and ripples to every corner of the earth.

The well-known Hebrew word for peace is *shalom*. Its root word means "whole" or "complete."

Peace comes not when there is diffusion or fragmentation, but when there is wholeness, fullness, and unity.

When a person feels solid at the core, when a person feels inner contentment and inner peace, there is little reason to engender confrontation or seek battle—at home, at work, in the world.

When Israeli Prime Minister Yitzhak Rabin and Jordan's King Hussein came to Washington, D.C. to sign the mutual recognition pact that ended the almost fifty-year state of war between their two countries, Rabin explained why this particular moment was ripe for peace.

He recalled that he had fought against Jordan in Israel's War of Independence in 1948. He was the army's Chief of Staff when Israel recaptured all of Jerusalem in the Six Day War of 1967. He was a member of government when Israel and Jordan did battle again in the *Yom Kippur* War of 1973.

Each time he went to war, it was with a burning passion to assure his country's existence and security—no matter what the price. And, he said, he knew that King Hussein watched him from across the border with the same fervent resolve for his own nation.

But now, Rabin said, both he and King Hussein are old men. The youthful idealism which led them to settle their differences on the battlefield has given way to the practical reality that warfare has settled nothing. Rabin related that as he looked into the eyes of his young granddaughter, he knew that he and his lifelong enemy must find a way for their countries to live in peaceful coexistence.

Countries do not make wars. Individual people do.

So now, with the peace that has come to the individual hearts of Yitzhak Rabin and King Hussein, peace can come to two great and powerful nations.

It is this same inner peace—the peace that you and your children can find and touch within the deepest and richest places of your beings—that can bring harmony to your world, your country, and the world of your institutions, your business, your work, your community, your friendships, your family, your most intimate relationships.

There is profound and enduring wisdom in the tale of the old sage who said, "When I was young, I prayed for the energy to change the world.

"In mid-life, I awoke one day and realized that my life was half over, and I had changed no one.

"So, I prayed for the energy to change those close around me—my family and friends, who needed it so much.

"Now that I am an old man, and my days are numbered, my prayer is much simpler. I pray, 'Oh, God, give me the strength to at least change myself.'"

When rightly perceived, the entreaty of the old folk song can be fulfilled by you and your children, "Let there be peace on earth. And let it begin with me."

A Story to Tell Your Children

The Pieces of Peace

Every night when a certain man came home from work, his children would run and jump into his arms, and ask, "Daddy, will you play with us? Please, Daddy, will you?"

And almost every night this man played with his son and his daughter, sharing games and books and toys.

One night, the father was very, very tired. So instead of rushing to play with his children, he sat down in a comfortable chair, opened his newspaper, and began to read.

As on every other night, his children asked, "Daddy, will you play with us tonight?"

But on this night, the man replied, "Oh, not tonight. I am so tired. I just don't have the strength to play with you tonight. You understand, don't you?"

The children did understand that their father was tired, but they really wanted him to play with them. So they kept asking. But their father's reply did not change.

Finally, to keep his son and daughter busy—and to get a little peace and quiet from their never-ending questions—the father took a whole page out of his newspaper. Printed on the page was a map of the whole world.

The father took a scissors and cut the map into many small pieces. Then he said to his children, "Here is a puzzle of the map of the world. Why don't you go and put the puzzle together?"

The father thought that the children would be gone for a long time, but they were back in just a few minutes.

The father was amazed, and he asked, "You finished the puzzle already? How did you do it? The map of the world is so large and difficult. How did you put it together so quickly?"

The little girl replied, "It was easy."

And her brother added, "On the back of the picture of the world was a picture of a person. We just put the person together, and the world fell right into place."

Questions to Discuss with Your Children About Peace

A Question to Discuss with Your Children (Ages 4–8)

You and your older brother or sister are always fighting. You think that s/he picks on you just because you are younger and smaller.

Or

You and your younger brother or sister are always fighting. You think that s/he always bothers you because you are older and bigger.

What do you do? What do you say to your brother or sister?
What do you say to your parents?

A Question to Discuss with Your Youngsters (Ages 9–12)

Two of your good friends are having a very bitter and continuing fight. Each one talks to you about the argument and complains about the other's faults. Each friend asks you to take his or her side.

What do you do? What do you say to each of your friends?

A Question to Discuss with Your Teenagers

Neo-Nazi skinheads, ranging in age from 15 to 22, have been caught distributing white supremacist literature on your high school campus. The same group of people is accused of defacing a local synagogue with swastikas and anti-Semitic graffiti.

You are asked by your school principal and the local chief of police to sit on an advisory committee—which will consist of teenagers and adults from the community—to determine the proper punishment for the skinheads.

Do you decide to sit on the committee? Why? Why not? What kind of punishment might you suggest for the skinheads?

A Prayer for Peace

Peace be in the heavens,
Peace be in the sky,
Peace be on earth,
Peace be in the waters,
Peace be in the plants and trees.

All is peace;
peace alone peace.

May that peace, real peace,
be with us all.

Peace, peace, peace
be unto us,
and to all the beings of the universe.

Sanskrit chant of the Atharva-Veda

The *9*TH

GOLDEN RULE

"Strive to Be a Man;
Strive to Be a Woman"

The Ethic of
MATURITY

More than fifteen hundred years ago, the Talmud—*a com-*
pendium of Jewish law and lore—taught that there are five
things which a parent must give a child.
    The first four requirements are readily understood.

1. *Parents must enter their children into a spiritual*
   covenant with God.
2. *Parents must provide their children with an educa-*
   tion—that is, give them the opportunity to gain
   knowledge and grow intellectually.
3. *Parents must teach their children a craft—that is, help*
   them learn to make a living.
4. *Parents must find a spouse for their children—for in*
   olden times, when marriages were arranged, it was the
   parents' task to find a suitable husband or wife for
   their daughters and sons.

    With slight adjustments for time and place, these four
obligations could be translated into equally valid parental re-
sponsibilities today.

But the Talmud's *fifth requirement seems very strange.*

1. Parents must teach their children how to swim.

To swim?

With all the profound and life-determining requirements that it makes, why does the *Talmud* insist that parents teach their children how to swim?

Parents are asked to give their children the tools with which to face any of the challenges or adversities that life will present.

For to know how to swim means to be able **to survive in a foreign and, sometimes, hostile environment.**

And parents are asked to learn a lesson about parenting.

For in teaching their children to swim, parents must know **how long to hold on and when to let go.**

Letting Go

The psychologist Haim Ginott put it most succinctly when he told parents about themselves and their growing children: "Our need is to be needed, and their need is to not need us."

After changing their dirty diapers and bandaging their scraped knees, after nursing them through their illnesses and guiding them through their studies, after soothing them in their fears and cheering them for their accomplishments, after catching their tears and rejoicing in their triumphs, after investing a lifetime of love and nurturing, it is hard for parents to admit that their little boy, their little girl, is growing up.

It is hard to accept Kahlil Gibran's fundamental truth that "your children are not your children. . . . They come through you but not from you. And though they are with you yet they do not belong to you."

Yet, every good parent knows that the job of parenting means giving children the gift of both roots *and* wings.

That is why every good parent would like to be able to under-stand—and relate to—this story.

The master had reached the outskirts of the village and settled down under a tree for the night when a villager came running up to him. "The stone," he said. "Give me the precious stone."

"What stone?" asked the master.

"Last night," the villager said, "the prophet appeared to me in a dream and told me that if I went to the outskirts of the village at dusk, I would find a master who would give me a precious stone that will make me rich forever."

The master looked in his bag and pulled out a stone. "He probably meant this one," he said. And he gave the stone to the villager, and said, "I found this in the forest a few days ago. You may certainly have it."

The villager took the stone and gazed at it in utter amaze-ment. It was a diamond—probably the largest diamond in the world, for it was as big as a man's head.

He took the diamond and walked away.

That night, he tossed and turned in bed, unable to sleep.

At dawn the next day, he quickly returned to the master. Waking him from his sleep, the villager beseeched the master, "Please, please. Give me the wealth that makes it possible for you to give away this diamond so easily."

You can give your children the gift of all their tomorrows when you can happily and confidently let them go.

What Will They Put in Their Suitcase and Who Will Ride in Their Spaceship?

When I was little—when space travel was still the stuff of comic books—I used to wonder whom I would take with me if I were sent on a spaceship to the moon. And I wondered what I would take along if I were permitted only one suitcase.

Undoubtedly, this was my youthful way of learning to make value judgments: who were the most important people and what were the most important things that I would want with me on a long, faraway journey?

From the day your children are born, you, their parents, are preparing for the day when your children will be grown and gone—when you must let them go.

So from the day your children are born, you can ask yourself, "What virtues, what values, what ideas, what ideals, what principles, what priorities do I want to give my children that they will, eventually, choose to pack up in their 'suitcase' when they are ready to leave?

"What are the measures of independence and maturity that I want to give to my children so that they can make it on their own—as competent, responsible, successful adults?

"What are the 'roots' that I want to deeply plant?"

Many parents' answers to these questions will be very similar, for they will be based on the universal values that are taught in this book. Some answers will be more personal, shaped by background, experience, and preference.

Every answer will start from the same place.

You want your children to be whole.

You want them to have the satisfaction that comes from stimulating work and gratifying play, from mutually interdependent relationships of caring and sharing, of loving and being loved.

You want them to know themselves and be true to themselves; to be inner-directed, focused, centered; to be solid and certain at their core; to be ever-evolving.

You want them to be in tune with their environment, in touch with their integrity, involved with their possibilities.

You want them to be connected and at one with the universe.

You want them to have serenity, contentment, and inner peace. You want them to share with their God the sacred task of balancing, transforming, and perfecting themselves and their world.

In his hit Broadway play and movie, *A Thousand Clowns,* Herb Gardner whimsically put it this way, "I just want him to stay with me 'til I can be sure he won't turn into a nothing. I want to be sure he'll know when he's chickening out on himself. I want him to know exactly the special thing he is, or else he won't notice when it starts to go. I want him to stay awake and know who the phonies are. I want him to know how to holler and put up an argument; I want a little guts to show before I can let him go. I want him to know it's worth all the trouble just to give the world a little nudge when you get the chance. And I want him to know the subtle, sneaky reason he was born a human being and not a chair."

You teach your children the measure of moral maturity when you convey to them your most precious values and your most cherished hopes for them.

Having Something to Do

You can teach your children that the measure of maturity is having something to do.

There was a man who died and found himself in a beautiful place, surrounded by every comfort.

A man in a white jacket came and said, "You may have anything you want—any food, any entertainment, any pleasure."

The man was overjoyed, and for days he sampled all the wonders of the place. He had every luxury that he had ever dreamed of or hoped for.

But one day, he grew bored with it all. He called the attendant and said, "I'm tired of all this. I need something to do, to keep me busy, to keep me occupied. What kind of work can you give me?"

The attendant shook his head and said, "I am sorry, sir. That is the one thing I cannot provide you. There is no work here for you."

Tuck Them In

When they are little—and they still let you—tuck your children into bed as often as you can.

When the sun sets and night comes, your children's fondest hopes, deepest thoughts, most troubling questions, and worst fears all come bubbling up to the surface of their consciousness.

When you make the time to tuck your children into bed, you are there to listen and to talk. You can hear their stories and tell them yours. You can help mold their ideas and beliefs and shape their feelings. You can wrap them in security and love with your tender hugs and gentle kisses.

When you tuck your children in at night, you are there to sing sweet songs and join together in quiet prayer; to soothe their bodies into sleep; and to accompany their souls into the magical world of imagination and dreams.

The man replied, "That's terrible. I might as well be in hell."

And the attendant quietly replied, "Where do you think you are?"

The old adage teaches, "We work not to acquire, but to become."

Yet, at the same time, you can teach your children that no matter how hard they work, no matter how old they become, they can never lose the child within them—their sense of wonder, of discovery, of playfulness. You can teach your children that the measure of maturity is to be not childish, but childlike.

Go Fly a Kite

When you fly a kite, or play a game, or toss a ball, or skip down the street, you show your children that play and fun and laughter are integral, vital parts of life for everyone—regardless of age or place.

When you play, you can show your children how to keep in touch with the childlike qualities of wonder and delight, imagination and creativity, and the ever-unfolding amazement and never-ending magic that is within them.

When you play, you show your children how to keep their lives in balance and their perspectives straight.

Having Someone to Love

You can teach your children that the measure of maturity is having someone to love.

One late autumn afternoon, a mother put her five-year-old son and his new-born baby sister on the front porch of their home to catch the last rays of the setting sun.

The little boy—impressed with the big responsibility his mother had given him—carefully guarded his tiny sister. The family dog—a wonderful, fluffy old mutt—stretched out contentedly and nuzzled close to the children.

A neighbor, observing the tender scene, called out to the little boy, and asked, "What are you doing?"

Without hesitation, the little boy replied, "I am loving them."

Henry Stack Sullivan taught, "When the satisfaction or the security of another person becomes as significant as one's own, then love exists."

You can teach your children that when you give yourself in love to your lover, to your children, to your parents, to your siblings, to your friends, you give the greatest gift you can give—the gift of self.

The author Saul Bellow put it simply, "A man is only as good as what he loves."

And you can tell your children that by giving love, they will, in turn, receive all the love they need.

Ovid put it best: "If you want to be loved, be loving."

And Rabbi Leo Baeck summed it up when he said, "The mark of a mature person is to give love and receive it joyously."

Having Something to Stand for

You can teach your children that the measure of maturity is standing up for principle—whatever the opposition, whatever the cost.

Only a generation ago, late-night college dorm room "bull sessions" were the place of passionate debate. Life—philosophy, history, literature, music, art, drama, sports, politics, social activism, religion, sex, anything and everything—was the subject; nothing was "off limits." Out of the heat of those encounters, young men and women forged their ideas, their ideals, and their principles.

Today—except in a few still enlightened and enlightening places—this generation's young men and women are hesitant to enter into debate, reluctant to display their passions; they do not want to challenge, do not want to contradict, do not want to offend. "After all," they say time and time again, "who is to say who is right? My friends are entitled to their own opinions, aren't they?"

You can teach your children that they can have—they need—principle and passion.

You can teach them the words of Jack Kerouac—the chronicler of that earlier generation—who said, "The only people for me are the mad ones, the ones who are mad to live, mad to talk, mad

LUMIE 43

Be a Designated Driver

You can most impress your children with your commitment to your convictions and your principles when you match your actions to your words.

If you tell your children not to smoke, then do not smoke. If you tell your children not to use drugs, then do not use drugs. If you tell your children not to drink, then do not drink.

If you tell your children that certain behaviors come with age and maturity, then use your age and maturity to show them moderation, control, and caution. If your friends drink, then you can be the designated driver to make sure that you all get home safely.

When you live your ideals, you show your children the importance of your moral choices and the sincerity of your decisions. Your children can then learn to honor their values and to keep the promises they make—responsibly and with determination.

to be saved . . . the ones who never yawn and say a commonplace thing, but burn, burn, burn, like fabulous yellow roman candles exploding like spiders across the stars."

A preacher said to his friend, "We have just had the greatest revival our church has ever had."

"Wonderful!" replied the friend. "How many people did you add to your church membership rolls?"

"None," said the preacher. "We lost five hundred."

A church that loses five hundred members rids itself of those who belong not out of conviction, but out of convenience. Those who remain stay because of belief and commitment, not because it is fashionable, popular, or easy.

LUMIE 44

Pay Your Taxes Gladly

No one likes to pay taxes. Everyone looks for every possible deduction and tries to find every legal loophole to reduce the amount of taxes to be paid.

But when you pay your taxes gladly, you show your children how to take their rightful place within their society and how to accept their obligations responsibly.

When you think about it, the taxes you pay are really a very small price for what you get in return—the privilege of living in a great land of democratic freedom and personal liberties. You get the protection of the military, police, fire, and emergency medical services. You get schools, libraries, highways, parks, and myriad public facilities and services.

When you pay your taxes gladly, you show your children how to appreciate the tremendous life blessings that are theirs and how to take their place as productive, accountable, dependable members of their community.

That is why the journalist Walter Lippmann taught, "A man has honor if he holds himself to an ideal of conduct even though it is inconvenient, unprofitable, or dangerous to do."

Having Something to Grow Toward

You can teach your children that the measure of maturity is having the capacity to continually grow.

Rabbi Bernard Raskas remembers that when the late, great Rabbi Mordecai Kaplan taught homiletics at the Jewish Theological Seminary, his custom was to explain the weekly scriptural reading at class on Monday in sermonic style.

The Ethic of Maturity   **167**

On Wednesday, a senior rabbinical student would present his version of the same biblical text in the same manner.

Dr. Kaplan was a very demanding and critical teacher, and the students dreaded their turn to recite.

Once, in class, a student took down verbatim what Dr. Kaplan said on Monday. On Wednesday, he repeated Kaplan's interpretation of the text, word for word.

When he was finished, Rabbi Kaplan said, "That was a terrible explanation of the text."

"But Dr. Kaplan," the student protested, "that's exactly what you said about the text on Monday."

And Kaplan replied, "Ah, yes, young man. But I have grown since then."

You can teach your children that the possibility of expanding their vision and enlarging their horizons is always theirs to grasp.

A woman dreamed that she walked into a new shop in the marketplace and, to her great surprise, found God behind the counter.

"What do you sell here?" she asked.

"Everything your heart desires," replied God.

"That is just wonderful," said the woman. "If that is so, then I want peace of mind and love and wisdom and happiness and freedom from fear." And, after a moment, she added, "Not just for me. For everyone on earth."

God smiled. "I think you have Me wrong, my dear," He said. "We don't sell fruits here. Only seeds."

God provides the raw materials of life. Your children can plant the seeds that will grow and flourish into the sweet and delicious fruits of their labors.

Being Satisfied

You can teach your children that the measure of maturity is being satisfied and content.

The ancient sage asked, "Who is rich?"

The answer he gave had nothing to do with wealth or material possessions.

"Who is rich? The one who is satisfied with his portion."

A wealthy businessman was horrified to see the fisherman lying lazily beside his boat, smoking a pipe.

"Why aren't you out fishing?" asked the businessman.

"Because I caught enough fish for one day," replied the fisherman.

"Why don't you catch some more?"

"What would I do with them?"

"You could earn more money," said the businessman. "Then with the extra money, you could buy a bigger boat, go into deeper waters, and catch more fish.

"Then you would make enough money to buy nylon nets. With the nets, you could catch even more fish and make more money.

"With that money you could own two boats, maybe three boats. Eventually you could have a whole fleet of boats and be rich like me."

"Then what would I do?" asked the fisherman.

"Then," said the businessman, "you could really enjoy life."

The fisherman looked at the businessman quizzically and asked, "What do you think I am doing now?"

You can teach your children that while there is great merit in "getting up and doing"—in being driven by their ambitions to achieve and accomplish—there is equally great merit in "sitting and doing nothing"—in appreciating and rejoicing in who they already are and what they already have.

A Quaker put up a sign on a vacant piece of land next to his home: THIS LAND WILL BE GIVEN TO ANYONE WHO IS TRULY SATISFIED

A wealthy farmer riding by saw the sign and said to himself, "Since our friend the Quaker is so ready to give away this land, I will claim it before anyone else does. I am already very rich and am very satisfied with all I have, so I meet the requirement to receive the land."

The farmer went to the Quaker's door and asked for the land.

"Are you truly satisfied?" asked the Quaker.

"I am," said the farmer, "for I have everything I need."

"My friend," said the Quaker, "if you are truly satisfied, then why do you want the land?"

You can teach your children the wisdom of the Zen saying: "Sitting quietly, doing nothing, spring comes, and the grass grows by itself."

The Measure of a Man; The Measure of a Woman

The story of the wandering prophet tells you—and your children—how to be the best kind of man, the best kind of woman.

The prophet once came to a city to teach its inhabitants to lead lives of goodness and worth.

At first, they listened to his sermons.

But gradually they drifted away until there was not a single soul to hear the prophet when he spoke.

One day a traveler said to him, "Why do you go on preaching?"

The prophet responded, "In the beginning, I had hoped to change these people. If I still shout, it is only to prevent them from changing me."

In modern times, Ralph Waldo Emerson defined the measure of the man, the measure of a woman, when he asked, "What is success?

"To laugh often and much; to win the respect of intelligent people and the affection of children; to earn the appreciation of honest critics and endure the betrayal of false friends; to appreciate beauty; to find the best in others; to leave the world a bit better, whether by a healthy child, a garden patch or a redeemed social condition; to know that even one life has breathed easier because you have lived. That is to have succeeded."

To give your children not only roots but wings, to give them the measure of their maturity and their success, you can teach them this simple yet profound dictum of the ancient sage, words that—when understood to include both genders—resonate through the centuries: "In a place where there are no men, strive to be a man."

A Story to Tell Your Children

The Stonecutter

Once upon a time, there was a stonecutter. Each day he went up the mountain to cut stones. And while he worked, he whistled and sang, for even though he was poor, he had no wish for anything more than he had. He was a happy man.

One day he was called to work at the mansion of a very rich man. When he saw the large and beautiful house, he felt a pang of desire for the first time in his life. He said, "If only I were rich. Then I would not have to earn my living with hard work and sweat."

Imagine how amazed the man was when he heard a voice saying, "Your wish is granted. From now on, anything you want will be given to you."

The man did not know what to make of the voice until he returned home that evening and found that, in place of his small hut, was a house as large and as beautiful as the rich man's.

So the stonecutter gave up cutting stones and began to live the life of the rich.

One afternoon, on a very hot day, he looked out his window and saw the king and all his noblemen going by. He thought to himself, "I wish I were a king myself, sitting in the cool comfort of a royal carriage."

No sooner had he made the wish than the stonecutter found himself riding in a cool, comfortable royal carriage.

But the day got hotter, and the carriage became warmer than the stonecutter ever imagined it could be. He looked out the carriage window and began to marvel at the power of the sun, whose heat could pierce through even the thick walls of the carriage. He said to himself, "I wish I were the sun."

Once again his wish was granted, and he found himself to be the sun, sending out waves of heat to the entire universe.

All went well for a while. Then, on a rainy day, the stonecutter—who was now the sun—tried to get through a thick bank of clouds. But he could not do it. So, he wished that he were a cloud, and, suddenly, he became a cloud, happy in his power to keep the sun away.

But soon, the cloud—who was really the stonecutter—felt himself being pushed by a great force. He realized that it was the wind, and so he said, "I wish I could be the wind." And, in a swift moment, he was the wind.

But it wasn't long before the wind blew up against something that even its great, powerful force could not move. It was a huge, towering stone, high on a mountaintop.

"That's it! I want to be a great, large stone," said the stonecutter, who was now the wind. And, in an instant, he was the stone, more powerful than anything on earth.

But, as he stood there in all his stony glory, he heard the sound of a hammer and chisel pounding into solid rock. "What could be greater than I, the greatest stone on earth?" he thought to himself.

So he looked down, and far below, he saw a stonecutter cutting chunks of stone from his feet.

And the stonecutter—who was now the great and powerful stone—said, "What? A tiny creature like that more powerful than a great rock like me? I want to be a man!"

So, before he knew it, the stonecutter was a man again.

And now, every day, he can still be found going up the mountain to cut stone—singing and whistling on his way.

Questions to Discuss with
Your Children About Being Grown Up

A Question to Discuss with Your Children (Ages 4–8)

You have a choice. You may have one ice cream cone today, and no ice cream cones all next week, or you may not have an ice cream cone today, but you may have one every day next week.

What do you choose? Why?

A Question to Discuss with Your Youngsters (Ages 9–12)

You want to do a lot of the things that your friends are doing—like hanging out at the mall, staying out late at parties, or buying very expensive "name-brand" sneakers.

Your parents tell you that you are "too young" for any of these things.

Other than telling your parents that "everybody" is doing it, how do you convince your parents that you should be permitted to do some of these things? If they still say no, what do you do?

A Question to Discuss with Your Teenagers

Your parents really want you to go to college—they've been dreaming about it and saving for it for years. You think college will be a waste of time, and you really want to go to a trade school that will prepare you for a career that really interests you.

Or

You are planning to go to college. You want to major in art history, because it is what really interests you. Your parents—who will be paying the bills—insist that you major in something "practical," like business or pre-med, so that you can get a good-paying job when you graduate.

How do you talk to your parents about what you want to do with your life? How do you get them to give up their dreams for you in exchange for your dreams for yourself? How do you assure them that you are making the right choices for your future?

A Prayer for
the Gifts of Maturity

*For the power to choose,
and the power to create,
we give thanks.*

*For the power to hope,
and the power to love,
we give thanks.*

*For the power to grow,
we give thanks.*

*For gifts beyond counting,
we give thanks.*

And we say, Amen.

Inspired by Rabbi Sidney Greenberg and
Rabbi Jonathan D. Levine;
adapted by W. D.

The Ethic of
FAITH

When I was in college, I took a philosophy course entitled
Writers on Ethics.

Professor Kendall King (that's really his name) assigned
the writings of more than a dozen philosophers attempting to
define the concept "good."

Each philosopher offered a different response, a different
definition, a different set of proofs. Every thinker's theories
and postulates were refuted by another. By mid-semester, my
classmates and I were confused, no closer to a working defini-
tion of "good" than when we had begun.

One day, Dr. King announced that after our long search,
he was finally going to provide the answer. He would give the
philosophical definition of "good." The date for the revelation
was a Friday afternoon, one week away.

Instantly, we realized that the announced date was the
last class session before spring break, and that the anticipated
proclamation was Kendall King's way of keeping us from
cutting class to begin an early vacation. But we eagerly fell
for the ploy because knowing the answer was important to us.

Not only was the professor's forthcoming definition a well-deserved reward for a half-semester's hard work and brain-wracking investigation, but each of us thought that we would be better educated, more enlightened, more complete human beings when we possessed the answer to this puzzling philosophical mystery.

The day arrived. We sat poised—notebooks open, pens in hand, as Dr. King strode into the room.

"Ladies and gentlemen," he said, "today we learn the answer."

With that, he turned to the blackboard and wrote, "Good is . . ."

We waited.

"Good is . . . good."

He turned back to us, set down the chalk, and said, "Have a very good vacation." And he walked out of the room.

The room erupted into an angry buzz. We were tricked; we were toyed with; we were used; we were abused.

And worst, we were still left without an answer. For this our parents were paying tuition? For this we were on an intellectual quest?

We left, feeling cheated of the extra vacation day we would have had if we had cut this silly class. And we left in a quandary, wondering, as the then-popular movie character Alfie wanted to know, "What's it all about?"

Only years later did I come to realize that not only was Kendall King a creative pedagogue, but that he was philosophically and intellectually honest.

He could not give a definition of "good" based solely on philosophical debate because philosophy has no ultimate definition of "good" that can stand objectively without being influenced by the subjective factors of *time, place, situation, personal whim, power, or charisma.*

What is good for me, may be bad for you. What is right for me, may be wrong for you.

For philosophy, there can be no other definition of "good" than "good is good."

Not Good Enough

But, you are not philosophical theorists.

You are human beings—parents, grandparents, aunts, uncles, babysitters, teachers, counselors, coaches, anyone and everyone who brings up and teaches children.

And you want a simple yet accurate way to define and know for yourself—and for your children—what is good and what is right.

You want to bring up children who have a solid ethical core, who know the difference between right and wrong, who make the right moral choice every time. You want children with a conscience.

Experts in child development teach that conscience—which will be tried, tested, examined, and matured all throughout childhood and adolescence—begins to develop at an early age.

The same experts also teach that it is not just the big moral dilemmas that help form conscience—for, after all, those momentous, life-changing situations arise only once in a while. Rather, a moral code is shaped and determined by the thousands of little decisions that a person makes every moment, every day.

And most importantly, they teach—but you already know this—**that your children's first and most important model of ethical behavior is you.**

Your children will develop their definitions of good and evil, their sense of right and wrong—their conscience—by listening to

your words, watching your actions, and seeing how you observe your ethical mandate hour after hour, day after day.

So, what will you teach your children?

What is good? What is right? What is wrong? What moral code, what standards of behavior, do you want your children to follow? What is the source of your morality and ethics?

Defining "Good"; Developing Conscience

You have philosophy's wide variety of choices from which to formulate your personal perception of "good."

Some will choose to define "good" from human reason: This kind of behavior makes logical, rational sense.

Others will choose to define "good" from human emotion: This kind of behavior makes me feel good.

Still others will choose to define "good" from societal norms: The consensus of our society agrees on this kind of behavior.

Still others will choose to define "good" from intuition: This kind of behavior seems right in my "gut," at the deepest core of my being.

And still others will choose to define "good" from a universal ethic: Everybody thinks that this behavior is right.

All of these systems of definitions have many positive aspects. But, each is equally flawed. Human reason, emotion, and intuition can all fail to think, feel, or sense the ultimate good; they can all be swayed to rationalize away the darkest evil. Societal norms and universal ethics can be distorted by evil people with evil purpose—Nazi Germany being the prime example.

All of these definitions of "good" are still subject to situation, circumstance, whim, caprice, or charisma—what philosophy calls "moral relativism," or "situational ethics."

Some may be lulled into embracing a popular—but significantly misunderstood—definition of "good."

From earliest childhood, parents tell their children to be "good" boys and girls.

Behave properly. Go to bed on time. Don't fight with your sister. Don't hit your brother. Be polite. Get good grades. Excel at what you do. Play to win. Hit a home run. Score the winning goal. Play your recital piece flawlessly. Have good friends. Get into a good college. Get good grades in college so that you can get into a good graduate school. Get a good job. Make good money. Choose a good husband or wife. Live in a good neighborhood. Drive a good car. Wear good clothes. Have good little children, whom you teach to be good, and who will start the cycle all over again.

But "good" is not determined by achievement or acquisition. All the accomplishments, all the material success, may mean doing *well.* **But, they do not mean doing** *good.*

Seeking the Source

In seeking the definition of "good," in seeking the source of conscience, many turn to the wisdom literature of the world's great spiritual traditions. For there is the record of humankind's encounter with enduring truths.

The noted author and radio talk show host Dennis Prager asks a striking question: If you were met by ten large, ominous-looking men, in a dark alley, late at night, wouldn't you be glad to know that they had just come from a Bible study class?

Ten large men? In a dark alley? Late at night?

I'd be frightened.

But almost immediately, I would feel a sense of relief.

Knowing that they learn and, hopefully, live the lessons of the Bible, I would assume that these men would not choose to harm me—for the Bible teaches us to do good, not evil, to do right, not wrong.

The problem is that sometimes—too many times—the

Study Sacred Texts

Sacred texts record the history of a faith community's search for and relationship with its God and its effort to understand and live by its God's teachings.

When you and your children learn from the holy writings of your own religious faith or ethnic tradition, you immerse yourselves in your own rich history and heritage.

When you learn from the holy writings of many different traditions, you find that while there is much that divides us as human beings, there is much, much more that unites us as children of the universe—and that there is much value and beauty in approaching the Divine in myriad ways.

"All the world," taught the sage, "is a narrow bridge. The main thing is not to be afraid." By reading and studying sacred texts with your children, you—and they—can find the way to cross the bridge into the place where the spirit of goodness dwells.

world's great wisdom literature has been perverted by the very people who claim to be its greatest proponents.

Instead of serving its intended purpose—as an inspiring, uplifting spiritual guide to goodness, righteousness, and moral excellence—it has been used as a weapon to control people's lives and induce their guilts.

Yet, when used properly—with reverence, joy, and a sense of ever-unfolding discovery—there is so very much to be gained from the collected wisdom of the ages.

As the Bible teaches, "The beginning of wisdom is this: Get wisdom!"

The Source of Conscience

A farmer, whose crop had done poorly, decided to "borrow" a few bushels of wheat from a neighboring farm.

On a dark and quiet night, the farmer and his eight-year-old son headed for a distant corner of the neighbor's field. They carried with them three large bushel baskets to fill with "borrowed" wheat.

When they reached the fence separating the two fields, the farmer looked carefully and furtively to the left and to the right, ahead of him and behind him. Just as he was about to step over the fence into the neighbor's field filled with an abundance of wheat, the tense silence was broken by the young boy.

"Daddy," he said, "you forgot to look up."

The little boy knew what his father had forgotten: there is a source and a power higher and greater than anything on earth, greater than any mastery or capacity that human beings have.

For many—if not most—people, the place where conscience is formed and from where it operates, the place where what is good and right is determined, is rooted in the world of the spirit, in the realm of the highest self.

For most, the ultimate source of conscience, the supreme definer of right and wrong, is God—in whatever form you conceive Him/Her/It to be.

This God—who created the universe and you—gave the ethical blueprint and moral mandate by which all humankind is to live.

Right is right and wrong is wrong not because of personal preference or opinion, but because God said so.

This God is not a stern law-giver who issues harsh orders, demands unquestioned obedience, metes out severe punishment, or invokes great guilt.

This is a God who sweetly, lovingly, and gently gives guidance and direction, who gives the gift of universal truths and enduring values, who gives the spark of Divine spirit to every heart and soul.

Seeking God

There was once a baby fish who swam up to his mother and asked, "Mom, what is this water that I hear so much about?"

His mother said, "Silly guppy. Water is around you and within you and gives you life. If you want to know what water is, just swim to the top of the pond and lie there for a while. Then you will find out what water is."

Another time, there was a little bear cub who walked over to her mother and asked, "Mom, what is this air that I hear so much about?"

Her mother said, "Silly little bear. Air is around you and within you and gives you life. If you want to know what air is, just stick your head in the stream. Then you will find out what air is."

Yet another time, a young man who was just beginning his spiritual quest, came to his parents and asked, "Mom, Dad, what is this God that I hear so much about?"

If you and your children want God as your source of conscience, you can seek Him/Her.

Once, a little girl was playing hide-and-seek with her friends. She hid herself in a dark, secluded spot, knowing that it would be very hard for her playmates to find her.

After waiting a long time, she came out of her hiding place, but her friends were nowhere to be seen. They had tired of the game and left her all alone.

The little girl began to cry, and she ran off to the comforting arms of her mother.

When her mother heard what had happened, she wiped her daughter's tears and said, "Do not weep, my precious child. Perhaps you can learn from this disappointment. All of life is like a game of hide-and-seek between God and us. Only it is God who is weeping. For God says, 'I am waiting to be found, but no one comes to seek Me.' "

A master was once asked, "Where is God?"

He replied, "God is everywhere—everywhere you let Him/ Her in."

Finding God

When God was ready to give commandments—the rules and regulations for human behavior—God went first—so the story goes—to the king of a great nation.

"I have some commandments to give you and your people," said God.

"What is one of the commandments?" asked the king.

"You shall not steal," replied God.

"Oh, I am sorry," said the king. "I would like to take Your commandments, but I cannot accept them. You see, my country's existence depends on how much we can steal from the nations and tribes around us."

So God went to the queen of another nation. "I have some commandments to give you and your people."

"What is one of the commandments?" asked the queen.

"You shall not murder," replied God.

"Oh I am sorry," said the queen. "I would like to take Your commandments, but I cannot accept them. You see, my country's existence depends on how many of our enemies we can kill."

So God went to the leader of one more nation and said, "I have some commandments to give you and your people."

This leader did not ask to hear one of the commandments. Instead, he asked, "Who are You?"

And God replied, "I am the Lord God who created you and your world, who caused the flood in Noah's time, and brought the Children of Israel from slavery in Egypt to freedom in the desert."

And the leader asked, "Why do You want to give us these commandments?"

And God replied, "Because I am your God, and you are My children. These commandments teach you, my precious children, how I want you to behave—to know the difference between right and wrong; to tell the truth and be honest; to treat each other with kindness and compassion."

And the leader of the people said, "We will take Your commandments, and we will try to follow them and come to understand them."

The leader knew what you and your children can know: **God's words can enter your being only when you are ready and open to receive them.**

There was once a very wise and learned man who went searching for the meaning of life.

After several years and many miles, he came to the hut of a holy hermit and asked to be enlightened.

The holy woman invited the man into her humble abode and began to serve him tea.

She filled the man's cup and then kept pouring and pouring, so that the tea overflowed the cup and was soon dripping on the floor.

The visitor watched as the holy woman continued pouring the tea, until he could no longer restrain himself. "Stop pouring. The cup is full. No more tea will go in."

And the sage replied, "Like this cup, you are full—full of your own ideas, opinions, and preconceptions. If you want me to teach you, you must first empty your cup."

By listening carefully for Divine words revealed to you in your time and place, you and your children can find God, create your own personal, intimate relationship with God, and come to know God's desires for you.

Then you can understand the old axiom that teaches, "To know God's will is life's greatest treasure. To do God's will is life's greatest pleasure."

Pray

When you and your children pray, you can talk to God and listen carefully as God talks to you.

You can thank God for all the blessings you have been given—life and health, the place you live, the food you eat, the clothes you wear, the good fortune that is yours. And you can ask God for the continued blessings that you hope, still, to receive.

You can ask God to be present in your life—giving help and protection, guidance and direction, wisdom and insight, hope and strength, comfort and support.

You can ask God to guide you to your life's purpose and mission. You can ask that God's word and will be continually revealed to you.

When you and your children pray—anywhere and everywhere, any time and all the time—you can hear God calling you to lives of goodness and righteousness.

Reflecting God

When you teach your children God's word, when your own words and deeds reflect your commitment to moral right, you transcend time and circumstance and enter into the world of the spirit—the world of being God-like.

God calls you to live a sacred life—embodying, imitating, and reflecting Divine being—"You shall be holy, for I the Lord am holy."

You and your children can internalize God's ethical values and set them as the core of your conscience.

Retreat

God is everywhere, and you can speak and listen to God any time you wish, but you and your children can make special times in special places to seek and find God.

Perhaps you will attend your church, synagogue, or mosque worship services, where in the quiet of the sanctuary, you can find your God.

Perhaps you will go to the seashore, the mountaintop, deep in the forest, or far out in the fields, where, in the majesty of nature, you can find your God.

Perhaps you will go on a retreat far away from your usual place, or, simply, retreat deep inside yourself to find your God in the "still small voice," and even in the sounds of silence.

When you and your children retreat, you intentionally make room for God in your life.

You and your children can—like God—do what is right and what is good.

You can teach your children that to follow their conscience, they need, first, a purpose for doing good.
Sometimes it seems as if the one who cheats, who lies, who looks the other way, who shades the truth just enough, is the one who prospers—who closes the deal, makes the sale, gets the raise, gets the promotion.

Sometimes it seems that not only—in the words of Rabbi Harold Kushner—do bad things happen to good people, but that good things happen to bad people.

Your children will see good, decent people who suffer, and they will see devious, hateful people who seem to thrive.

They will wonder why there does not seem to be a direct correlation between behavior and reward or punishment. And they will be struck by the seeming random capriciousness of the universe.

They will be moved to ask what good there is in doing good.

But then they will see—as you did before them—the temporal, fleeting nature of momentary reward. They will begin to wonder what the wealth, the possessions, the fame—whether gotten by ill gain or well earned and well deserved—ultimately mean.

They will hear the voice of Elizabeth I—surrounded by all her great wealth—calling through the centuries, "All my possessions for a moment of time." Your children will understand—as the queen did—that when time runs out, even the greatest fame and fortune cannot be carried down to the grave.

So your children will soon be moved to ask another question: What do I gain by doing good, by committing my life to honesty and integrity, to fairness and justice, to compassion and sharing, to reaching out beyond myself to touch and affect the lives of others?

And they will hear the voice of Erich Fromm telling them that "[doing] good is all that serves and enhances life."

And they will hear the voices of time telling them, in the words of the modern prayer, that there is "purpose to their work, meaning to their struggle, and direction to their striving."

Your children can know that when they do good, they will feel better about themselves, that their humanity will be affirmed, that life will ultimately be better, richer, more ennobling, more deeply satisfying.

And you can teach your children that to follow their conscience, to do good, they need commitment.

In this age of instant gratification, some people do good for as long as it feels good, and then, no more.

They volunteer to help, until the task interferes with their own plans or until something better comes along.

They take on a cause, until the cause is not as popular as it once was.

They throw away relationships, friends, marriages, alliances when they become too troublesome or inconvenient.

You can teach your children—as you have already learned—that they cannot be content with volunteering today, for there is still work to be done tomorrow.

They cannot be content with telling the truth today, for their honor and their reputation is still at stake tomorrow.

They cannot be content with feeding hungry people today, for there will still be people who are hungry tomorrow.

They cannot be content with doing good today, for there is so much good that needs to be done tomorrow.

You can teach your children that to do good means to make a commitment for today, for tomorrow, for every day.

To do good means to do good forever.

And you can teach your children that to follow their conscience, to do good, they need courage.

The glib advertising seems to make it so easy for your children: "Just say no!"

But it is not easy for them—or for us—with drugs or any other tempting allure.

It is never easy to say "no," and really mean it.

It is never easy to say "yes," and really mean it.

There *are* temptations. There *are* unspoken expectations. There *are* pressures and stress and undue influence.

It is hard to do good in a society that celebrates doing well; to do good without promise of remuneration or reward; to do good

Count Your Blessings

Despite its many challenges and disappointments, despite its painful episodes and its hurtful encounters, your life—and the lives of your children—is filled with many blessings—blessings you know and blessings that are still to be revealed to you.

You can help your children appreciate and celebrate their life and their many blessings—and the source of their blessings—when you literally count your blessings.

When you take a piece of paper and make a list, you and your children can see how very many blessings of goodness you have, and how richly and strongly you are supported.

When you show your children how much good they have, you can teach them how to give thanks to the source of their blessings, and you can help give them the inner fortitude to face adversity when they must.

When you count your blessings, you can say to yourself and your children, "Blessed am I. Blessed are you."

when others are doing what is popular, what is prevalent, what is easy; to do good just for its own sake.

But, your children—as you did before them—can do good if they have courage.

And they can do good because their courage comes from that hidden inner place that drives them, that enflames them, that gives them their passions.

And your children can know—as you knew before them—that the place, the core, within them that creates the spark is God—God within them leading them to God-directed goodness;

God within them leading them to God-directed holiness; God within them leading them to be like God.

As the old axiom teaches, "As it is above, so it is below."

In Partnership with God

The biblical proverb teaches, "Train a child in the way he should go, and even when he is old, he will not depart from it."

George Benson explains: "Great ideas and fine principles do not live from generation to generation just because they are good, nor because they have been carefully legislated. Ideals and principles continue from generation to generation only when they are built into the hearts of children as they grow up."

That is why an old legend insists that at the moment of a child's conception, *three* are present—the mother, the father, and God.

In bringing a precious soul to earthly existence, a partnership is formed between God and the parents.

God provides the ultimate spark of life, and, then, gives the blueprint—the moral mandate of ethical values—of how life is to be lived.

The parents become the stewards and the caretakers of the soul, gently and lovingly providing their child with guidance and direction according to Divine plan.

You have been given the great and glorious privilege and responsibility of guiding your precious children to lives of goodness and righteousness, decency, and worth.

Rabbi Kassel Abelson reminds you that the Hebrew word for *parents* and the Hebrew word for *teacher* come from the same root. You are the first and the most important teacher your children will ever have.

That is why the psychologist Bruno Bettelheim taught, "Above all, children need adults whose behavior makes sense, who live a consistent set of values, and after whose image they can form a personality."

John Costello adds, "If a child is going to internalize our values, the child must know what our values are. They must be spelled out for him in words and deeds."

The holy *Koran* explains your parental role perfectly when it teaches you how to bring up your children: "The purpose of man's creation is that he should become a manifestation of God's attributes, in other words, the image of God."

Measure for Measure

An old adage teaches, "Conscience is like a sundial—when the truth of God shines upon it, it points the right way."

When you teach your children to live God's truths, they—like you—will want to do what is right and what is good.

And they—like you—will want to find a way to measure their conduct, to know whether they have really done right.

For—when you teach them goodness and right—they will well understand the chilling reality of the Japanese proverb: "The reputation of a thousand years may be determined by the conduct of one hour."

In the light of day, your children want to be able to stand proud and certain.

And in the dark of night, they want to be able to sleep soundly and fearlessly.

And in the quiet of eternity, they want to be able to face their God.

And in all these places, truth is the only currency.

In all these places, some will hear the shout or the whisper of God's voice speaking to them.

Some will feel an intuitive sense in their "gut," at the deepest core of their being.

Some will have a highly developed sense of conscience, of spirit, calling out to them.

Some will truly understand the words of the great artist Michelangelo, painting frescos in the Sistine Chapel.

Lying on his back high up on a scaffold, he very, very carefully was outlining a figure in a corner of the ceiling.

A friend asked, "Why do you take such meticulous care with a figure so high up in the ceiling, so many feet above where the viewer will be standing? After all," continued the friend, "who will know whether or not the figure is perfect?"

And Michelangelo replied, "I will."

The technology of the modern age gives you one more question to ask your children, one more way for them to measure and evaluate their conduct:

What if your every word and every deed of today were being recorded on a hidden video camera?

When the tape is played on tomorrow night's six o'clock news for the whole world to see, will you be proud and excited, or embarrassed and humiliated?

The age-old notion of the all-seeing, all-knowing God is given a new—and starkly real and immediate—dimension.

The Heart of the Matter

One day, a young man became an apprentice to a blacksmith.

The smith was a very fine teacher, and he showed the young man everything he knew about being a blacksmith—how to use the bellows to keep the fire hot; how to use the tongs to take the metal from the fire; how to use the hammer and anvil to shape the shoe; how to talk gently to the animals; how to nail the shoe to the horse's foot.

After a number of years of careful training, the blacksmith said to his young apprentice, "I have now taught you everything I know about being a blacksmith. You are now a fine and talented smith yourself. The time has come for you to leave me and open your own blacksmith shop."

The young man followed his teacher's advice and went to the next town to open his shop.

Write an Ethical Will

No matter how much or how little you have, you will probably write a will, leaving your possessions and your financial resources to your children.

But you have something much greater and, ultimately, much more valuable to give your children. You can leave your children your ethical and spiritual legacy.

When you write an *ethical* will, you can talk to your children from the Great Beyond and tell them the ideas, the ideals, the beliefs, the values, the people, and the relationships that are important to you.

Not that you want to "haunt" your children or leave them with unreasonable expectations or unwanted guilts. You simply— and profoundly—can bequeath to them your most precious spiritual values, your heritage of goodness, your inheritance of love.

With current technology, you can enhance your ethical will by using audio or video tape to record it, so that your children can have not just the message, but the image of the messenger.

When you leave an ethical will, your values will live on in your children, and your children will treasure your greatest gift.

A few months later, the master smith journeyed to see how his young student was faring.

He came to a fine-looking shop, where he found the new young blacksmith surrounded by all the finest equipment.

But the kiln was cold, the bellows were silent, the hammer and tongs hung unused, and no horses were to be found.

The master said to his student, "What is wrong? I was sure that you would have plenty of business in this fine new shop. But you have no customers, there are no horses in the stalls, and you are not making even one horseshoe. Didn't I teach you well? Didn't I show you how to be a good blacksmith?"

The young man looked sadly at his mentor and said, "Master, you taught me very well. You taught me how to use the bellows and the tongs, the hammer and the anvil; you taught me how to make the shoes and put them on the horses.

"There is only one thing you failed to teach me. You never taught me how to light the fire."

Parents—teachers, mentors, masters—when you teach your children how to light the fire of conscience, when you teach them how to warm themselves by the fires of God, then you teach them to understand and embrace the words of President John F. Kennedy in his inaugural address: "With a good conscience as our only sure reward, with history the final judge of our deeds, let us go forth . . . asking His blessing and His help, but knowing that here on earth, God's work must surely be our own."

A Story to Tell Your Children

Your Very Own Angel

In the High Heavens lives an angel named Lailah, who has a very special job.

The High Heavens are full of souls who spend their time being very close to God, learning all the secrets of the universe.

But, as wonderful as it is in the High Heavens, every soul longs to come to earth to have the adventure called life.

When it is time for a new baby to be born, Lailah searches and searches throughout all the High Heavens to find the right soul, and to help it choose for itself the most perfect parents on earth.

During the nine months that the soul is in the womb of its mother, Lailah watches over it and reminds it of all that it has learned in the High Heavens—all the wisdom and the secrets of the universe, all the love it felt being so close to God.

But souls cannot be born into human form with all the knowledge of the universe, because then life would not be such an adventure.

So just as your soul—now in your body—is to be born, Lailah taps the baby (that's you!) on your upper lip, leaving that little indentation right under your nose.

With this gentle touch, you forget all the knowledge and secrets of the whole universe, but keep just enough wisdom and understanding to be a human being on earth.

Every now and then, you may hear a sound or see a glimmer of something you think you remember and that might be one of the secrets that you once knew but have now forgotten.

And every now and then, if very wise people—like your mother or your father, or your sisters or brothers—know the right questions to ask you, maybe, just maybe, you might be able to remember one of the secrets and be able to tell it.

And every now and then, throughout your whole life—no matter how wonderful your life is—you may feel—in the deepest part of your heart—that something is missing. Maybe everyone who has ever lived feels this way. Maybe everyone misses the High Heavens and misses being so close to God.

And so part of the adventure called life is about finding ways for your soul to feel as close to God here on earth, as you did when you were a soul in the High Heavens.

And Lailah, the angel, knows that. So she remains a guardian of your soul, watching over you and protecting you all your days, helping you to feel close to God and being happy when you remember the secrets.

If you remember any of the secrets, now is the time to tell.

Questions to Discuss with Your Children About God

A Question to Discuss with Your Children (Ages 4–8)

Your grandparents are visiting. They tell you that at the end of their visit, there will be "very special treats" for everyone who has been a "good little boy or girl."

What does it mean to you to be a "good" boy or girl? What do you think it means to your grandparents?

A Question to Discuss with Your Youngsters (Ages 9–12)

You feel close to God all the time, especially since your parents told you that God is everywhere. But your parents insist that you go with them to church, synagogue, or mosque to pray to God there.

You think that the services are boring, and you see many people there talking with each other instead of praying. But you know that your parents feel good about attending services and really "get something out of it."

What do you say to your parents about your feelings? How do you get your parents to respect your beliefs?

A Question to Discuss with your Teenagers

Tragedy has struck your school. A very talented and popular senior has been killed in a car crash. In their shock and grief, many of your friends turn to their faith in God for comfort and consolation. Other friends say, "That's it. I've had it with God! How can I believe in a loving, caring, good God who lets this happen?"

What do you think God's role is in this tragedy? What does this tragedy do to your faith in God? What do you say to your friends on both sides of the issue?

A Prayer to God

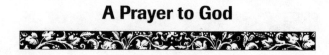

*God be with us,
as You were with our ancestors.*

*Open our hearts,
so that we may walk in Your ways,
and observe Your laws and teachings.*

*May we love You,
and serve You with fullness of spirit,
this day and every day.*

Amen.

King Solomon's prayer at the Dedication of
The Holy Temple, 1 Kings 6:57–59;
adapted by W. D.

The Extra-Special Bonus

Create a Memory Bank

Every word you and your children speak, every action you and your children take, every deed you and your children perform is indelibly printed in your cells and on your soul, just as if they were being recorded on a continually running film or tape.

Together—every moment, every day—you and your children are creating their "memory bank."

When you speak sweet and gentle words, when you perform worthy and righteous deeds, when you always act out of goodness, kindness, and decency, you create pleasant and positive memories for your children—memories on which they will build and sustain their lives.

You give your children a priceless gift—the greatest investment in their future—when their memory bank contains your most precious values, your enduring sense of right and wrong, and your most cherished dreams.

The memory bank you create for your children is their permanent record. It is your history and your posterity. It is their inheritance and their destiny.

Make your deposits wisely and well.

One More Story
to Tell Your Children

The Monks

High in the mountains was a monastery that had once been known throughout the world. Its monks were pious, its students were enthusiastic. The chants from the monastery's chapel deeply touched the hearts of people who came there to pray and meditate.

But, something had changed. Fewer and fewer young men came to study there; fewer and fewer people came for spiritual nourishment. The monks who remained became disheartened and sad.

Deeply worried, the abbot of the monastery went off in search of an answer. Why had his monastery fallen on such hard times?

The abbot came to a guru, and he asked the master, "Is it because of some sin of ours that the monastery is no longer full of vitality?"

"Yes," replied the master, "it is the sin of ignorance."

"The sin of ignorance?" questioned the abbot. "Of what are we ignorant?"

The guru looked at the abbot for a long, long time, and then he said, "One of you is the messiah in disguise. But, you are all ignorant of this." Then, the guru closed his eyes, and he was silent.

"The messiah?" thought the abbot. "The messiah is one of us? Who could it be? Could it be Brother Cook? Could it be Brother Treasurer? Could it be Brother Bell-Ringer? Could it be Brother Vegetable Grower?

"Which one? Which one? Everyone one of us has faults, failings, human defects. Isn't the messiah supposed to be perfect? But, then, perhaps these faults and failings are part of his disguise. Which one? Which one?"

When the abbot returned to the monastery, he gathered all the monks together and told them what the guru had said.

"One of us? The messiah? Impossible!"

But, the master had spoken, and the master was never wrong.

"One of us? The messiah? Incredible! But, it must be so. Which one? Which one? That brother over there? That one? That one?"

Whichever one of the monks was the messiah, he was, surely, in disguise.

Not knowing who amongst them was the messiah, all the monks began treating each other with new respect. "You never know," they thought, "he might be the one, so I had better deal with him kindly."

It was not long before the monastery was filled with new-found joy. Soon, new students came to learn, and people came from far and wide to be inspired by the chants of the kind, smiling monks.

For once again, the monastery was filled with the spirit of love.

To best remember the story of the monks, here is:

A Poem to Learn
with Your Children

If you will always assume
the person sitting next to you
is the messiah
waiting for some human kindness,

You will soon learn to weigh your words
and watch your hands.

And if he so chooses
not to reveal himself
in your time,

It will not matter.

A Rebbe's proverb
translated by Danny Siegel

A Prayer for the World

Where there is hatred, may I bring love.
Where there is pain, may I bring healing.
Where there is darkness, may I bring light.
Where there is despair, may I bring hope.
Where there is discord, may I bring harmony.
Where there is strife, may I bring peace.

Make this a better world. And begin with me.

Inspired by St. Francis of Assisi;
adapted by W. D.

And Let Us Say . . .

He said, "Come to the edge."
And they said, "We are afraid."
She said, "Come to the edge."
And they said, "But, we will fall off."
He said, "Come to the edge."
And they came to the edge.
And she pushed them off.

And then, they began to fly.

. . . Amen

THE LUMIE LIST

Here they are: all FIFTY LUMIES to help you teach your ethical values to your children.

LUMIE 1
Eat Breakfast

LUMIE 2
Praise People

LUMIE 3
Speak Love; Show Love

LUMIE 4
Visit the Elderly

LUMIE 5
Visit the Cemetery

LUMIE 6
Play "Telephone"

LUMIE 7
Play "Truth or Dare"

LUMIE 8
Take Your Children to Work

LUMIE 9
Return Library Books

LUMIE 10
Check Your Check

LUMIE 11
Play Board Games

LUMIE 12
Don't Yell at the Umpire

LUMIE 13
Have a Pillow Fight

LUMIE 14
Turn Off the Television

LUMIE 15
Turn On the Television

LUMIE 16
Vote

LUMIE 17
Volunteer

LUMIE 18
Have a Block Party

LUMIE 19
Visit a Sick Friend

LUMIE 20
Give Blood

LUMIE 21
Fast

LUMIE 22
Contribute

LUMIE 23
Have a Family
"Piggy Bank"

LUMIE 24
Work in a Soup Kitchen

LUMIE 25
Give Away a
Pair of Socks

LUMIE 26
Take a Walk

LUMIE 27
Take a Hike

LUMIE 28
Witness a Birth

LUMIE 29
Plant a Garden

LUMIE 30
Go to a Museum

LUMIE 31
Take a Course

LUMIE 32
Be a Mentor

LUMIE 33
"Make New Friends,
but Keep the Old"

LUMIE 34
Create New Traditions

LUMIE 35
"Root, Root, Root for
the Home Team"

LUMIE 36
Have Family Meetings

LUMIE 37
Meditate & Mediate

LUMIE 38
"Cast Your Bread upon the Waters"

LUMIE 39
Demonstrate

LUMIE 40
Turn Off the Television— Again

LUMIE 41
Tuck Them In

LUMIE 42
Go Fly a Kite

LUMIE 43
Be a Designated Driver

LUMIE 44
Pay Your Taxes Gladly

LUMIE 45
"Whistle a Happy Tune"

LUMIE 46
Study Sacred Texts

LUMIE 47
Pray

LUMIE 48
Retreat

LUMIE 49
Count Your Blessings

LUMIE 50
Write an Ethical Will

LUMIE 51
Create a Memory Bank

SOURCES

Biblical quotations are taken from Tanakh, The Holy Scriptures: A New Translation According to the Traditional Hebrew Text *(Jewish Publication Society, Philadelphia, 1985) or from the author's own translation of the original Hebrew. Quotations from* Pirkay Avot *are taken from* Sayings of the Fathers, *edited by Joseph H. Hertz (New York: Behrman House, 1945) or from the author's own translation of the original Hebrew.*

Introduction

"In the Beginning"
GENESIS 1:1

"From where will your help come?"
AFTER PSALMS 121:1

"all your heart, all your soul, all your might."
DEUTERONOMY 6:5

"If not now, when?"
AVOT 1:14

The First Golden Rule

"Honor Your Father and Your Mother"
EXODUS 20:12

"O Lord, the world is filled . . ."
PSALMS 8:1

"When I see the heavens . . ."
PSALMS 8:4

"You have made us almost Divine. . . ."
PSALMS 8:6

"You shall rise before the aged."
LEVITICUS 19:32

"Your young shall dream dreams . . ."
JOEL 3:1

The Second Golden Rule

"Be Heedful of Your Words"
AVOT 1:9

"Do What Is Right"
DEUTERONOMY 6:18

"The truth shall make you free."
JOHN 8:32

"Guard my tongue . . ."
FROM THE JEWISH PRAYERBOOK;
AT THE CONCLUSION OF THE *AMIDAH*

The Third Golden Rule

"Justice, Justice Shall You Pursue"
DEUTERONOMY 16:20

"Lord, open his eyes . . ."
II KINGS 6:17

"Do not look at the container . . ."
AVOT 4:27

"With the judgments you make . . ."
MATTHEW 7:2

"the person who shames another in public . . ."
B. TALMUD, BABA METZIA 58B

"It is not your task . . ."
AVOT 2:21

"All that we have heard . . ."
AFTER EXODUS 24:7

The Fourth Golden Rule

"Do Not Separate Yourself from the Community"
AVOT 2:5

"If I am not for myself . . ."
AVOT 1:14

"Every human being is responsible. . . ."
BASED ON, "ALL ISRAEL IS RESPONSIBLE . . ."
B. TALMUD SHEUOTH 39A

The Fifth Golden Rule

"Let the Poor Be Members of Your Household"
AVOT 1:5

"Give Your servant..."
I KINGS 3:9

"When he needed only one portion..."
KOHELET RABBAH 7:30

"gracious and compassionate..."
AFTER EXODUS 34: 6-7

The Sixth Golden Rule

"Consider the Marvelous Works of God"
JOB 37:14

"How great are Your works..."
PSALMS 104:24

"You shall not say in your heart..."
DEUTERONOMY 8:17

"... But the earth has been given..."
PSALMS 115:16

"If you are planting..."
AVOT DE RABBI NATAN 31

"Of the making of books..."
ECCLESIASTES 12:12

The Seventh Golden Rule

"Get [Yourself] a Teacher and Acquire [for Yourself] a Friend"
AVOT 1:6

"I have learned much..."
B. TALMUD TA'ANIT 7A

The Eighth Golden Rule

"Dwell Together in Unity"
PSALMS 133:1

"Cast your bread..."
ECCLESIASTES 11:1

"I cry 'Peace, Peace..."
AFTER JEREMIAH 6:14

The Ninth Golden Rule

"[In a Place Where There Are No Men] Strive to Be a Man"
AVOT 2:6

The Tenth Golden Rule

"You Shall Be Holy"
LEVITICUS 19:2

"The beginning of wisdom . . ."
PROVERBS 4:7

"still small voice"
JOB 4:16

The stories told in this book—both the stories interspersed throughout the chapters and the stories to tell children—are part of the great oral tradition of storytellers, teachers, and preachers throughout the generations. I have listened to many of these stories since earliest childhood, and I have told them over the past thirty years and more. Some of the same stories are part of many ethnic and religious traditions—internalized, particularized, and retold as the story of a specific group. All of them have one goal—to convey a universal value in a sweet but powerfully dramatic way. Many of the stories of the oral tradition have been collected into books, with many stories—in their various forms—often appearing in two, three, and more books. Grateful acknowledgment is made to these books, which set down the stories of the oral tradition, and which have been consulted to assure a story's origin and accuracy.

Allison, Christine. *Teach Your Children Well: A Parents' Guide to the Stories, Poems, Fables and Tales That Instill Traditional Values.* A John Boswell & Associates Book, Delacorte Press, New York, 1993.

Certner, Simon, ed. *101 Jewish Stories: A Treasury of Folk Tales from* Midrash *and Other Sources.* Board of Jewish Education of Greater New York, New York, 1961.

Cleary, Thomas. *Zen Antics: 100 Stories of Enlightenment.* Shambhala, Boston & London, 1993.

———. *One Minute Wisdom.* Image Books Doubleday, New York, 1988.

de Mello, Anthony. *The Song of the Bird.* Image Books, Doubleday, New York, 1984.

———. *Taking Flight.* Image Books, Doubleday, New York, 1990.

———. *The Heart of the Enlightened.* Doubleday, New York, 1989.

Dosick, Wayne. *The Business Bible: Ten New Commandments for Creating an Ethical Workplace.* William Morrow & Co., New York, 1993.

Feldman, Christina, and Jack Kornfield. *Stories of the Spirit, Stories of the Heart.* HarperSanFrancisco, a division of HarperCollins, New York, 1991.

Frankel, Ellen. *The Classic Tales: 4,000 Years of Jewish Lore.* Jason Aronson Inc., Northvale, New Jersey, 1989.

Polsky, Howard W., and Yaella Wozner. *Everyday Miracles: The Healing Wisdom of Hasidic Stories.* Jason Aronson Inc., Northvale, New Jersey, 1989.

Raskas, Bernard S. *Heart of Wisdom.* The Burning Bush Press, New York, 1962.

———. *Heart of Wisdom Book II.* The Burning Bush Press, New York, 1979.

————. *Heart of Wisdom Book III.* The United Synagogue Commission on Jewish Education, New York, 1986.

Schwartz, Howard. *Gabriel's Palace: Jewish Mystical Tales.* Oxford University Press, New York and Oxford, 1993.

Wharton, Paul J. *Stories and Parables for Preachers and Teachers.* Paulist Press, New York, 1986.

White, William R. *Stories for the Journey.* Augsburg Publishing House, Minneapolis, 1988.

The attributed quotes in this book—although all in the public domain—have been collected into various books. Grateful acknowledgment is made to the authors and editors of these books for gathering this wisdom.

Alcalay, Reuven. *Words of the Wise.* Masada Press, Jerusalem, 1970.

Andrews, Robert. *The Concise Columbia Dictionary of Quotations.* Avon Books, New York, 1987, 1989.

Brown, David. *Bible Wisdom for Modern Living.* Simon and Schuster, New York, 1986.

Davis, Rebecca, and Susan Mesner. *The Treasury of Religious Quotations: Words to Live By.* Reader's Digest, Pleasantville, New York, 1994.

Fields, Rick. *Chop Wood, Carry Water: A Guide to Finding Spiritual Fulfillment in Everyday Life.* Jeremey P. Tarcher, Inc., Los Angeles, 1984.

Fitzherny, Robert I. *The Harper Book of Quotations.* HarperPerennial, a division of HarperCollins, New York, 1993.

Gibran, Kahlil. *The Prophet.* Alfred A. Knopf, New York, 1966.

Griffith, Joe. *Speaker's Library of Business: Stories, Anecdotes and Humor.* Prentice-Hall, Englewood Cliffs, New Jersey, 1990.

Keen, Sam, and Anne Valley-Fox. *Your Mythic Journey: Finding Meaning Through Writing and Storytelling.* A Jeremy P. Tarcher/Putnam Book, G. P. Putnam's Sons, New York, 1973, 1989.

Levine, Mark L., and Eugene Rachlis. *The Complete Book of Bible Quotations.* Pocket Books, New York, 1986.

Mieder, Wolfgang. *The Prentice Hall Encyclopedia of Word Proverbs.* Prentice-Hall, Inc., Englewood Cliffs, New Jersey, 1986.

Miller, Ronald S., and The Editors of *New Age Journal.* *As Above So Below: Paths to Spiritual Renewal in Daily Life.* Jeremy P. Tarcher, Inc., Los Angeles, 1992.

Newman, Louis I. *The Talmudic Anthology: Tales and Teachings of the Rabbis.* Behrman House, New York, 1945.

Pentz, Croft M. *The Complete Book of Zingers.* Tyndale House Publishers, Inc., Wheaton, Illinois, 1990.

Prochnow, Herbert V. *Speaker's & Toastmaster's Handbook.* Prima Publishing, Rocklin, California, 1993.

Raskas, Bernard S. *Living Thoughts: Inspiration, Insight and Wisdom from Sources Throughout the Ages.* Hartmore House, New York & Bridgeport, 1976.

Safire, William, and Leonard Safir. *Good Advice: More Than 2,000 Quotations to Help You Live Your Life*. Wings Books, New York, 1982.

Schiller, David. *The Little Zen Companion*. Workman Publishing, New York, 1994.

Van Ekeren, Glenn. *Speaker's Sourcebook II: Quotes, Stories & Anecdotes for Every Occasion*. Prentice-Hall, Englewood Cliffs, New Jersey, 1994.

Zona, Guy A. *The Soul Would Have No Rainbow If the Eyes Had No Tears: And Other Native American Proverbs*. Simon and Schuster, New York, 1994.

The prayers to recite with your children in this book have all been adapted by the author from prayer ideas, words, or kernels appearing in these books. The original prayer-writer who inspired the prayer is credited with each prayer. Grateful acknowledgment is made to all the men and women who give us beautiful and moving new words with which to approach our God in prayer.

Appleton, George, ed. *The Oxford Book of Prayer*. Oxford University Press, 1985.

Boyd, Malcolm. *Are You Running with Me Jesus?* Avon Books, New York, 1965.

Brin, Ruth. *Harvest: Collected Poems and Prayers*. The Reconstructionist Press, New York, 1986.

Greenberg, Sidney, and Jonathan D. Levine. Mahzor Hadash: *The New* Mahzor *for* Rosh HaShanah *and* Yom Kippur. The Prayer Book Press, New York and Bridgeport, 1978.

Greenberg, Sidney, and Jonathan D. Levine. Siddur Hadash: *Worship, Study and Song for Sabbath and Festival Mornings*. The Prayer Book Press, New York and Bridgeport, 1991.

Harlow, Jules. Siddur Sim Shalom: *A Prayerbook for* Shabbat, *Festivals and Weekdays*. The Rabbinical Assembly and The United Synagogue of America, New York, 1985.

Roberts, Elizabeth, and Elias Amidon, eds. *Earth Prayers from Around the World: 365 Prayers, Poems and Invocations Honoring the Earth*. HarperSanFrancisco, a division of HarperCollins, New York, 1991.

Silverman, Morris, ed. *Sabbath and Festival Prayerbook*. The Rabbinical Assembly of America and The United Synagogue of America, New York, 1946.

Van de Weyer, Robert, ed. *The HarperCollins Book of Prayers: A Treasury of Prayers Through the Ages*. HarperSanFrancisco, a division of HarperCollins, New York, 1993.

Grateful acknowledgment is made to these authors—and to the ideas in their books—who have done recent work in the field of bringing up ethical children. These books are warmly recommended for those who seek further study of the issues discussed here in Golden Rules.

Ames, Louis Bates. *Raising Good Kids*. A Delta Book, Dell Publishing, New York, 1992.

Bennett, William, J., ed. *The Book of Virtues: A Treasury of Great Moral Stories.* Simon and Schuster, New York, 1993.

Coles, Robert. *The Moral Life of Children.* Houghton Mifflin Co., Boston, 1986.

Coles, Robert. *The Spiritual Life of Children.* A Peter Davison Book, Houghton Mifflin Co., Boston, 1990.

Edelman, Marian Wright. *The Measure of Our Success: A Letter to My Children and Yours.* Beacon Press, Boston, 1992.

Eisenberg, Nancy. *The Caring Child.* Harvard University Press, Cambridge, 1992.

Eyre, Linda, and Richard Eyre. *Teaching Children Joy.* Ballantine Books, New York, 1980.

———. *Teaching Children Responsibility.* Ballantine Books, New York, 1982.

———. *Teaching Your Children Values.* A Fireside Book, Simon and Schuster, New York, 1993.

Glenn, H. Stephen, and Jane Nelsen. *Raising Self-Reliant Children in a Self-Indulgent World: Seven Building Blocks for Developing Capable Young People.* Prima Publishing, Rocklin, California, 1989.

Hayes, E. Kent. *Why Good Parents Have Bad Kids: How to Make Sure That Your Child Grows Up Right.* Doubleday, New York, 1989.

Kilpatrick, William. *Why Johnny Can't Tell Right from Wrong: And What We Can Do About It.* A Touchstone Book, Simon and Schuster, New York, 1993.

Kurshan, Neil. *Raising Your Child to Be a Mensch.* Atheneum, New York, 1987.

Louv, Richard. *101 Things You Can Do for Our Children's Future.* Anchor Books, Doubleday, New York, 1994.

Reuben, Steven C. *Raising Ethical Children: 10 Keys to Helping Your Children Become Moral and Caring.* Prima Publishing, Rocklin, California, 1994.

Schulman, Michael, and Eva Mekler. *Bringing Up a Moral Child: A New Approach for Teaching Your Child to Be Kind, Just and Responsible.* A Main Street Book, Doubleday, New York, 1985.

Shapiro, Rami M. *The One Minute Mensch.* EnR Wordsmiths, Inc., Miami, 1985.

Wolpe, David J. *Teaching Your Children About God.* Henry Holt, New York, 1993.

An outstanding resource for guidance in writing an ethical will is:

Riemer, Jack, and Nathaniel Stampfer, eds. *So That Your Values Live On: Ethical Wills and How to Prepare Them.* Jewish Lights Publishing, Woodstock, Vermont, 1991.

INDEX

Guardian angel, 195–96

Ha'am, Ahad, 40
Heedless words, 29–30
Hiking, 102
Honesty: consequences of not being, 35–37; dealing with, 33–35; discussion questions on, 43; evolving consciousness of, 38–40; practicing, 37–38; prayer on, 44; public scrutiny of, 40; story for children on, 41–42; taught by example, 27–28
Howe, E. W., 130
Hugo, Victor, 109
Hussein, King, 153–54
"Hyman Dosick cherry rule," 34–35

"In Your Hands" (children's story), 60–61

Judging, 51–53
Justice: affirmed through behavior, 55–56; for all people, 47–48; equality and, 49–50, 58–59; judging vs., 51–53; prayer for, 62; prejudice vs., 50–51; through service, 56–58. *See also* Fairness

Kaplan, Rabbi Mordecai, 167–68
Kennedy, John F., 56
Kerouac, Jack, 165
Kindness. *See* Compassion
King, Kendall, 176–78
King, Martin Luther, Jr., 56, 59
Kushner, Rabbi Harold, 187

Learning: continuation of, 119–23; through experience, 123–26. *See also* Friends
Library books, 38
Lincoln, Abraham, 37
Lippmann, Walter, 167

Love: children's story on, 200–201; speaking/showing, 18
Loyalty, 132–33
LUMIES: on bedtime, 163; on block parties, 71; on board games, 47; on breakfast time, 14; on "casting bread," 149; on cemetery visits, 22; on contributions, 84; on counting blessings, 190; described, 6–7; on educational courses, 121; on family meetings, 143; on family "piggy bank," 85; on family traditions, 130; on friends, 128; on garden planting, 108; on giving blood, 74; on good sportsmanship, 49; on hiking, 102; on library books, 38; listed, 205–7; on love, 18; on loyalty, 133; on meditate & mediate, 147; on memory banks, 199; on mentors, 126; on museum visits, 110; on paying taxes, 167; on peace demonstrations, 151; on pillow fights, 54; on positive attitudes, 170; on praising people, 16; on prayer, 186; on restaurant check, 39; on retreats, 187; on scripture study, 181; on socks, 90; on soup kitchens, 88; on taking children to work, 36; on teaching by example, 166; on "Telephone" game, 31; on "Truth or Dare," 34; on TV, 58, 152; on value of playing, 164; on visiting the elderly, 20; on visiting sick friends, 73; on volunteering, 69; on voting, 68; on walks, 101; on witnessing birth, 104

Malice, 29–30
Mandela, Nelson, 56
Maturity: childlike wonder within, 163–64; children's story on, 172–73; contentment within,